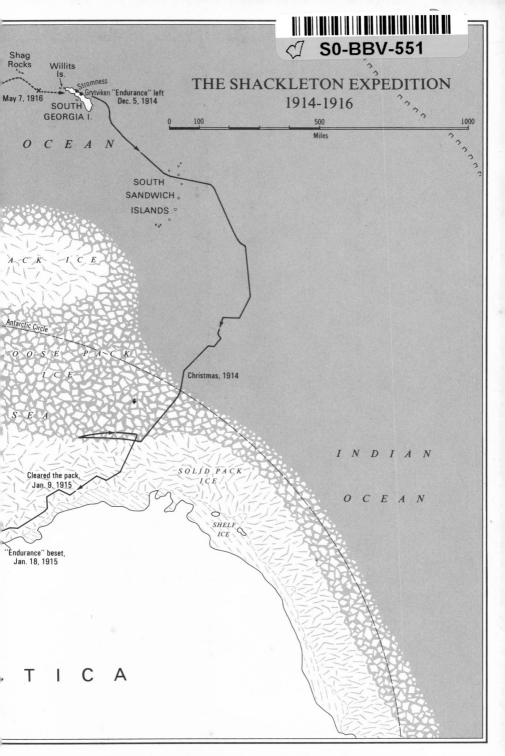

THE SHACKLETON EXPEDITION
1914-1916

SHACKLETON'S BOAT JOURNEY

G.W. Biggers
December 1977

SHACKLETON'S BOAT JOURNEY

F. A. WORSLEY

Narrative Introduction by

SIR EDMUND HILLARY

W·W·NORTON & COMPANY·INC·

New York

Copyright © 1977 by W. W. Norton & Company, Inc.
Published simultaneously in Canada by George J. McLeod
Limited,
Toronto. Printed in the United States of America.

First Edition

Library of Congress Cataloging in Publication Data

Worsley, Frank Arthur, 1872–1943.
Shackleton's boat journey.

1. Antarctic regions. 2. Shackleton, Ernest
Henry, Sir, 1874–1922. I. Title.
G850 1914.W63 1977 919.8'9'040924 [B] 76-53808
ISBN 0-393-08759-X

This book was designed by Jaques Chazaud
Typefaces used are Perpetua and Baskerville,
Manufacturing was done by Haddon Craftsmen.

2 3 4 5 6 7 8 9

Contents

5

Illustrations

Illustrations

8

Members of the Expedition

Sir Ernest Shackleton	*Leader*
Frank Wild	*Second in Command*
Frank A. Worsley	*Captain of Endurance*
H. Hudson	*Navigating Officer*
L. Greenstreet	*First Officer*
T. Crean	*Second Officer*
A. Cheetham	*Third Officer*
L. Rickenson	*Chief Engineer*
A. Kerr	*Second Engineer*
J. A. McIlroy	*Surgeon*
A. H. Macklin	*Surgeon*
R. S. Clark	*Scientist*
L. D. A. Hussey	*Scientist*
J. M. Wordie	*Scientist*
R. W. James	*Scientist*
G. Marston	*Artist*
T. Orde-Lees	*Motor Expert*
F. Hurley	*Photographer*
W. McNeish	*Carpenter*
T. Green	*Cook*
A. Blackborrow	*Steward*
J. Vincent	*AB*
T. Macarty	*AB*
A. How	*AB*
A. Bakewell	*AB*
T. McLeod	*AB*
H. Stephenson	*Fireman*
A. Holness	*Fireman*

9

Introduction

I would venture to guess that if a survey were carried out in America about Antarctic explorers it would be found that most young people would be familiar with the local hero, Admiral Richard E. Byrd; many would know that Roald Amundsen was first to the South Pole; and some might even have heard vaguely of Captain Robert Falcon Scott. But I doubt if anyone except a student of Antarctic literature would recognise the name of Sir Ernest Shackleton, who to my mind was at least the equal of them all. Lasting fame is a fragile thing—it has often little to do with the magnitude of the achievement but rather with being fortunate enough to do the right thing at the right time—or to die in sufficiently romantic circumstances to capture the imagination of the public.

Most of us have a hero or two that we openly or secretly admire, even if we cannot always explain why one particular person should have greater appeal to us than anyone else. Do we sometimes choose our heroes because they are larger-than-life versions of our own aspirations and abilities? Certainly in the sphere of Antarctic exploration I have always had a great admiration for Sir Ernest Shackleton—and even after my own share of adventures in the Southern Continent I still retained the conviction that of all the explorers I would like to have known, Shackleton was the most admirable. The reading I have done of old diaries and new books in order to write this introduction has only confirmed this opinion.

And yet Shackleton, great explorer though he was, could probably be regarded as unsuccessful on all his major journeys—if success is judged solely by the limited standard of whether a set goal has been achieved. It was as a leader of men and an overcomer of appalling obstacles that Shackleton really excelled. Not for him an easy task and a quick success—he was at his best when the going was toughest. The enormous affection and respect he engendered in his expedition members (often mighty men themselves) shines through in their diaries and writings.

Shackleton's first trip south was as a lieutenant in Captain Scott's famous *Endeavour* expedition in 1901–1904. The team was a rather unusual combination of Royal Navy, merchant navy, and scientists. One of the younger members, Reginald Ford, acted as Scott's secretary on the voyage. Ford later settled in New Zealand and became a principal of a distinguished Auckland architectural partnership. I was fortunate enough to become a good friend of the elderly Ford and was frequently enthralled by his stories of the *Endeavour* expedition.

He told me how difficult Scott had found his dealings with the merchant navy personnel, who were not accustomed to the rigid discipline of the Royal Navy. One merchant seaman in particular was most reluctant to accept orders and was regarded as a very bad influence on the rest of the crew. Scott decided that he would have to be sent back on the first relief vessel. Reginald Ford and Shackleton were present when Scott advised the seaman that he was being sent home. To Scott's absolute astonishment the seaman refused to be repatriated—he had signed a contract and knew his rights—he was staying on to the end of the expedition whatever Scott might think. Ford related how Scott simply didn't know how to handle the situation —the man after all was not subject to naval discipline.

Then Shackleton, a merchant navy officer, asked permission to deal with the problem. Scott agreed and departed from the cabin—but Ford stayed on. Shackleton calmly informed the seaman that he was returning to Britain—the man insolently disagreed—so Shackleton, a powerful man, stepped forward and knocked him to the deck. The man rose slowly to his feet and Shackleton gave him his instructions once again. Somewhat more slowly and much less arrogantly the man refused. Once again the man was flattened by a mighty blow. When he got up this time and realised that Shackleton was prepared to carry on the procedure indefinitely he was happy to agree to an immediate departure. Ford ended his days with an overwhelming admiration for Shackleton both as a man and as a leader and I have no reason to question the truth of his story. No doubt it was a brutal answer to a difficult problem but it was still a brutal age and Shackleton undoubtedly understood his men—he could be as gentle as a woman and incredibly considerate of his crew's welfare, or as tough as was required to deal with any problem.

In many respects the *Endeavour* expedition was not a happy one for Shackleton. Scott chose him with Dr. Edward Wilson to make up the three-man team to push south towards the Pole, so he must have felt considerable confidence in Shackleton's abilities. And yet it turned into a most terrible journey for all of them. They headed south over the Ross Ice Shelf with a good deal of confidence but their nineteen dogs gradually weakened and became useless because of tainted food and they were forced to largely manhaul their supplies for day after day—frequently doing long periods of relaying, as not all their loads could be pulled in one effort. They were soon further south than anyone had been before and each day new mountains, inlets, and headlands could be seen to the southwest. Their own strength was gradually ebbing as they carried on with their exhausting work on very limited rations. Scott and Shackleton were also showing ominous signs of scurvy.

At $82°16'$ south, after nearly sixty days of enormous effort, they agreed they could go no further—they were 238 miles closer to the Pole than anyone had been before. Their journey back to McMurdo Sound became increasingly desperate as their scurvy intensified, and Shackleton was short of breath, coughing and sometimes spitting blood. Gradually all the dogs were destroyed and they reduced their loads to the absolute minimum for manhauling. They were at the very end of their strength when they rounded White Island and could see the sharp cone of Observation Hill—and knew they were safe at last!

Scott seemed to feel that Shackleton had let the party down by his illness, even though conceding that it must have been as annoying for Shackleton as it was for himself. Shackleton had been very ill indeed and Scott decided to send him home with the next relief ship. This was a bitter disappointment to Shackleton and undoubtedly hardened his resolve to return again with his own expedition.

It was not until the beginning of 1907 that Shackleton formally announced his expedition. His objectives were an extensive scientific programme, a number of long exploratory trips, and a determined effort to reach the South Pole. He did not have government backing and the raising of finance proved an almost insuperable obstacle. He was forced to economise in every direction and make do with a tiny vessel—the *Nimrod,* of 200 tons. But despite the lack of official support and finance, Shackleton's reputation as a leader was shown by the quality of the men he was able to gather around him—people such as Douglas Mawson, Raymond Priestly, Professor Edgeworth David, and Frank Wild, all to become redoubtable names in Antarctic exploration.

Shackleton took some dogs with him but had little confidence in their ability, after his previous experience. Instead he intended to use tough Manchurian ponies plus the traditional manhauling. They established their base on Cape Royds, as Scott had refused permission for them to use the old *Discovery* hut. Before the onset of winter a party made the ascent of the 13,370-feet-high active volcano Mt. Erebus and looked down into its steaming crater for the first time.

The winter at Cape Royds seemed a very happy and profitable one, with all members of the party sharing the general duties—a change from Scott's expedition, where the separation of the officers and lower decks was more pronounced. As early as August 12, the party took turns at sledging journeys and gained experience at living and working hard under very cold temperatures.

Shackleton had brought south a motor car for towing sledges and it was hoped that this would share the work of the ponies, many of which had already died from accident or food poisoning. But although some useful work was carried out by the car, Shackleton regretfully decided that it would not cope with the soft snow conditions on the Ross Ice Shelf.

The main journey south began on October 29, 1908, but right from the start they struck problems with deep snow, crevasses, and bad weather. Shackleton was already worrying about their food supply—they had planned on supplies for ninety-one days but in the first eleven days they had only made fifty-one of the 1,760 miles they had to go if they were to reach the Pole and return. Conditions improved a little and Shackleton, Adams, Marshall, and Wild, plus their four ponies, made their way steadily south. On November 19 they were at 80°32' south and it gave them heart to know that Scott, Shackleton, and Wilson had been almost a month later getting to this point, even though they had left at almost the same time. But one of their ponies was making poor progress and had to be shot on the twenty-first and the load shared up amongst the remaining three ponies. The animals were all getting very tired and the men were too.

November 22 was a superb day and to their great excitement they saw new land—"great snow-clad heights"—rising beyond Mt. Longstaff, the furthest south land seen on the 1902–1903 march. "It is a wonderful place we are in," wrote Shackleton, "all new to the world, and yet I feel that I cannot describe it. There is an impression of limitless solitude about it all that makes us feel so small as we trudge along, a few dark specks on the snowy plain, and watch the new land appear."

On November 26 they had passed Scott's furthest point south and they were a month ahead in time. They were mostly in good shape and the three remaining ponies were pulling well despite frequent stretches of soft snow. But they were still over 500 miles from the Pole—and the high land was still ahead of them. Their hopes for an easy gateway to the Pole were rapidly declining—they would have to cross the mountains.

"South of us a glacier opens up," wrote Wild, "leading through the mountains in an almost south direction, and so . . . at lunch it was decided to make for that, climb a mountain, and see how the land lies." From the top of Mt. Hope—3,350 feet—they saw with joy "a great inland sea of ice stretching as far as eye could see, and flanked by magnificent mountains."

And so commenced their fearful battle with the giant Beardmore Glacier. Crevasses were everywhere and suitable snowy spots to camp precious few. On the fourth day their last pony disappeared forever down a giant crevasse and Wild nearly went with it—but he and the vital sledge were saved.

Day after slogging day the four men hauled the two sledges, with their combined weight of 1,000 pounds —and every day death was just around the corner. Shackleton recorded it in his diary:

December 8: ". . . dodging crevasses and pits of unknown depth."

December 9: "Marshall was only saved by his harness. He had quite disappeared down below the level of the ice. . . . soon after Adams went through, then I did."

December 10: "Falls, bruises, cut shins, crevasses, razor-edged ice, and a heavy upward pull."

And so it went on. . . .

They were cutting back on their already minimal rations but time was running against them and still the glacier went up and up. They were hoping desperately for a levelling out, a polar plateau, but it never seemed to come. On December 23 Shackleton wrote "Eight thousand eight hundred and twenty-five feet up, and still steering upwards amidst great waves of pressure ice and icefalls, for our plateau . . . was not the plateau after all."

I have flown down the shattered length of the Beardmore Glacier in a comfortably heated aircraft

and despite the fact that I myself had spent a genera-
tion of climbing up and down glaciers and falling into
crevasses I marvelled that those gallant pioneers
should have persisted in their unbelievable efforts—
not knowing what the next day might bring, always
being short of food, always uncomfortable, and realising that their chances of return were deplorably slim
—but still going on.

I wonder how our "hard men" of today with their
fancy equipment and "instant rescue" by radio and
helicopter would have survived under such conditions? Danger is one thing, but danger plus extreme
discomfort for long periods is quite another. Most
people can put up with a bit of danger—it adds something to the challenge—but no one likes discomfort—
or not for long, anyway. I expect that even in our
comfort-orientated society there are always a few
tough and hardy souls who are prepared to make these
efforts.

Altitude started affecting Shackleton's party. On
January 1 they were 10,757 feet above sea level and
still nearly 200 miles from the Pole. They had "three
weeks food and two weeks biscuit" to get to the Pole
and back to the last depot. It is clear that even Shackleton was realising that their chances of success were
now very slim. On January 3 Wild wrote "We have
now come to the conclusion that we cannot get to the
Pole, so tomorrow we are making a depot of sufficient
food and oil to take us back to our last depot at the
head of the glacier at half rations." They now planned
a last rush with ten days' food and one tent.

But the surface and the wind were against them—

19

for two days of "blinding, shrieking blizzard" they made no advance at all. On January 9 they realised their push was finished. The wind had died down a little and at 4 A.M. they left their camp with no sledge, and half walking and half running they carried on until 9 A.M. to reach 88°23' south—111 statute miles (97 nautical miles) from the South Pole—and here they planted their flag. It had been a phenomenal effort by remarkable men.

The journey back was a desperate race against dwindling rations and strength. They were helped by the tail wind and made some excellent distances. On January 25 they covered twenty-six miles down the glacier but after they had finished dinner that night they had food left for only one more meal. "If we should happen to have a thick day tomorrow I don't suppose anyone would ever have the chance of reading this" wrote Wild in his diary.

On the twenty-sixth they had their last food, a panniken of "hoosh," and from then on there was nothing but a scrap of chocolate and tea or cocoa. On the twenty-seventh they camped exhausted half a mile from their Depot D at the foot of the glacier. Marshall went on to collect some food, breaking through three crevasses on the way. But "Never did men enjoy a meal more" was written on his return.

But still they were operating on the slimest of margins. Wild developed dysentery and a blizzard held them up for most of the day. Wild was getting worse and Shackleton now developed dysentery himself.

On the night of January 31 Wild wrote: ". . . [Shackleton] privately forced upon me his one breakfast biscuit, and would have given me another tonight had I allowed him. I do not suppose that anyone else in the world can thoroughly realise how much generosity and sympathy was shown by this: I do, and by God I shall never forget it. Thousands of pounds would not have bought that one biscuit."

As they struggled their way back over the Ross Ice Shelf Shackleton and Wild recovered their health but they were all still on verge of starvation. By the time each depot was reached they had exhausted the food supplies they were towing. On February 23, with Erebus in sight, they reached the last depot that had been laid for them and their food problems were over. There was news too about their ship, the *Nimrod,* which had arrived on January 5—but would it still be there? It was now Marshall's turn to become very sick with dysentery and it was all he could do to stagger along, let alone help with the hauling. Shackleton decided he would leave Adams to care for Marshall while he and Wild pushed on with a single day's food. In a quite astonishing effort of endurance they walked an estimated ninety miles with only three hours sleep. There was no sign of their ship at the *Discovery* hut but finally they saw it in the distance and were able to attract its attention. At 11 A.M. on March 1 they were on board.

Not satisfied with this effort, 3 1/2 hours later on the same day Shackleton set off back with a relief party to bring in Adams and Marshall. He had everyone safely on board ship on March 4. Shackleton had kept going for six days with only a total of fifteen hours rest after an incredibly tough journey of 1,700 miles. No wonder his companions held him in such respect.

The trip towards the Pole was not by any means the only great journey undertaken by Shackleton's party. There were numerous long treks of exploration and many hazardous adventures. The most noteworthy was that of Professor David, Douglas Mawson, and Dr. Mackay, who carried out a tremendous manhauling journey to become the first men to reach the South Magnetic Pole. When the *Nimrod* arrived back in New Zealand they received a rapturous welcome and the acclaim of the world.

The years 1910 to 1913 were the peak years of the classical era of Antarctic exploration. Amundsen, in masterly fashion, reached the South Pole with his dog team on December 16, 1911. A month later—January 17, 1912—Scott and his party manhauled their way to the Pole—and died on the return journey.

After Amundsden's success in reaching the Pole, Shackleton concluded that "there remained but one great main object of Antarctic journeyings—the crossing of the South Polar continent from sea to sea." His plans were extensive and complex. One ship, the *Endurance,* would go south from Buenos Aires in October 1914 and land Shackleton's six-man crossing party and eight other men on the Weddell Sea coast at 78° south in November. He hoped that if all went well the crossing would be commenced immediately and completed in the same season. If they were delayed by too many problems they would carry out reconnaissances to the south and depots would be laid for a crossing in the summer of 1915–1916. Shackleton had worked out that the actual journey would take a maximum of five months.

A support ship, the *Aurora,* would enter the Ross Sea on the other side of the continent and establish a base on Ross Island. From there a party of six men would proceed south along the traditional route, laying depots, and hope to meet the crossing party at the head of the Beardmore Glacier. Even the outbreak of war in Europe on August 4, 1914, did not put a stop to the expedition, as the British Admiralty insisted it go ahead.

In fact, the crossing never took place. Shackleton's ship, the *Endurance,* was gripped by the heavy pack ice in the Weddell Sea and his party never set foot on the Antarctic continent. The *Endurance* was finally crushed by the ice and sank, and all the efforts of Shackleton and his party were devoted to survival. The great crossing of the continent was left to Sir Vivian Fuchs more than forty years later. I had the job of establishing a base in McMurdo Sound and laying out depots for Fuchs's party; and having done that we carried on to become the first people to drive vehicles overland to the South Pole. I had done an initial trip into the Weddell Sea with Fuchs in the 800-ton sealer *Theron.* We too became well and truly stuck in the pack ice, so I had some comprehension of Shackleton's problems —except that his party were completely and utterly alone and dependent on their own resources. In a more technical age we had continuous radio communication with the outside world, a small aircraft that could operate off water or snow for aerial reconnaissance, and always the possibility that an icebreaker or helicopters might be able to get through to our aid. Even so it was a trying enough experience, as our steel ship creaked and groaned under the pressure of the ice. How must Shackleton and his men have felt?

Once again Shackleton was supported by men of remarkable quality. Frank Wild, his deputy leader, had proved himself time and again a man of incredible courage and tenacity. Shackleton had chosen Frank Arthur Worsley as skipper of the *Endeavour.* Worsley was born at Akaroa in New Zealand in 1872 (I had always admired Worsley but until I came to write this introduction I had not realised that he was a fellow New Zealander). He had a pioneering upbringing, typical of the New Zealand of his day. He helped his father clear the bush and graze hundreds of sheep on the new pastures. He seems to have been a difficult pupil at school until he struck a principal who understood his character and potential. Although he was frequently beaten, "never once had I cried, whimpered, endeavoured to evade punishment, or told a lie," which would certainly make him unique amongst his present day compatriots. He ended up by becoming head boy of the school.

Because of his small size he felt the need to excel and when he became an apprentice on square-rigged ships no risk was too great for him to take when he was up in the rigging. Somehow he survived his enthusiasm for taking chances and, by the time Shackleton signed him on as master of the *Endurance,* he was an exceptionally tough and able seaman, forty-three years old, and perhaps most important of all, a brilliant navigator. His courage, strength, and spirit of adventure had automatically attracted him to Shackleton and he gave the same unswerving loyalty and devotion as did Frank Wild. What a tremendous trio they were to face any eventualities!

The *Endurance* was gripped immovably in the Weddell Sea on January 18, 1915, in temperatures that were exceptionally cold for that time of the year. For ten months the ship and its crew drifted to the north until the enormous pressure exerted on the hull crushed it in and the vessel sank on November 21, 1915. As if this was not enough, the sinking of the *Endurance* initiated what must undoubtedly be one of the most remarkable stories of survival in recorded history. For five months the whole ship's party of twenty-eight drifted north on a huge ice floe—an ice floe that shattered and shrank as time passed. No man could sleep at night and expect to wake safe in the morning. Cracks opened up under tents; camps had to be changed with desperate speed; and killer whales were cruising in any open water. I have had a killer whale rise up beside me as I stood on a chunk of floating ice and can remember the singularly unsympathetic look in its beady eye—my retreat to the ship was unquestionably precipitate.

Shackleton displayed his superb leadership during this very trying period—keeping everyone busy, making alternative preparations for any eventualities, and maintaining morale with jokes, entertainments, and special treats. His spirit never seemed to flag, although his diary reveals his deep concern for the men and their situation. One evening he even cheerfully discussed taking an expedition to Alaska when the present one was finished. Worsley remarked, "We look up all the maps and books on the subject that we can lay our hands on and are enthusiastic about our next trip before we can definitely settle how the devil we are going to get out of this one. . . ." (I know the reaction well from my own experience.)

The long period of relative inactivity on the ice floes demanded enormous patience from Shackleton and was possibly the most difficult period for him to bear, as he normally revelled in action and adventure. The three boats saved from the *Endurance* were in a constant state of readiness in case the ice should split apart, as it inevitably must do. During January, February, and March the surface of the ice floes was soft and mushy and living was continuously wet and uncomfortable, with an increased sense of insecurity and appalling boredom. But somehow Shackleton held the group together, displaying caution when caution was needed, and never permitting his firm control to slacken.

And then on April 8 a crack opened up underneath one of the boats, splitting the camp in two. It was time for action! On April 9 the pack ice separated and the boats were quickly launched. Then followed seven days of constant crises and danger as they jostled through the rest of the pack ice and finally out into the wild open seas to an ultimate landing on April 15 on desolate Elephant Island.

So Shackleton had his men on solid land once more —helped by the unshakeable Wild, by Worsley in navigation, by the spirit of every man in the crew, and by his own unflinching determination not to be beaten.

One of the party, Macklin, summed it up as well as anyone: "I think his taking of those overloaded boats through the ice, with seventeen hours of darkness in the twenty-four, breaking up and grinding of floes, and the whole set of conditions of the seven days we were in the boats, constituted a truly remarkable piece of leadership."

But still they were only on Elephant Island—a desolate speck in Antarctic waters—and nobody had any way of knowing they were there. They clearly must rescue themselves.

And so was undertaken their great ocean voyage. Shackleton's largest boat was only twenty-two feet six inches long and he had ahead of him probably the stormiest ocean in the world. Where should he go for help? The prevailing winds were fierce westerlies—so the only possible way was to sail to the east. Eight hundred miles away was the mountainous island of South Georgia and there were some whaling stations there, but if they missed the island it would be the end for them all—that's if they hadn't already been swamped by the mountainous seas.

As was to be expected, Shackleton decided to lead the rescue attempt himself. Worsley too was an essential choice, with his great experience of the sea and his exceptional ability as a navigator. Four other tough men were added to make up a crew of six. Frank Wild remained behind to keep the other twenty-two survivors alive on Elephant Island.

Worsley's account of that journey is a breath-taking story of courage, skill, and determination under the most appalling conditions. Not only were the seas a mighty problem but the incredible discomfort must have been almost unbearable. It is impossible not to admire the skill of Worsley in taking advantage of the few glimpses they had of the sun to fix their position and navigate the boat to a landfall on the southwest coast of South Georgia. It took them sixteen days of wild and furious weather and it must have been tremendous to be on solid land again.

But the whaling stations were on the other side of the island—and half of Shackleton's crew were disabled, and their boat was no longer seaworthy. They would have to cross on foot. Many years later, I observed from the *Theron* with admiration and enthusiasm the beautiful ice-clad mountains of South Georgia; but Shackleton and his men must have regarded them in quite a different light—they were a formidable barrier between themselves and safety.

The three incapacitated members had to wait behind for rescue while Shackleton, Worsley, and Crean set off across glaciers and snowy passes, frequently being turned back by impossible terrain but fumbling on through cloud and wind. After thirty-six hours of mighty effort they struggled into the whaling station at Stromness for a warm welcome, and safety at last. Shackleton's thoughts turned immediately to the men left on Elephant Island. Winter was on them and the pack ice forming fast. The first three attempts to get to Elephant Island were unsuccessful, but finally on August 30, 1916, Shackleton broke through and found all twenty-two of his men safe and well.

The "Boss," as Shackleton was called, had not failed

28

them and once again not a man had been lost. It only confirmed the view of his friends that Shackleton was "the greatest leader that ever came on God's earth, bar none."

Auckland, New Zealand   EDMUND HILLARY
June 28, 1976

SHACKLETON'S BOAT JOURNEY

PART I

From the Endurance
to
Elephant Island

I

The Weddell Sea might be described as the Antarctic extension of the South Atlantic Ocean. Near the southern extreme of the Weddell Sea in 77° south latitude Shackleton's ship *Endurance,* under my command, was beset in heavy pack ice. The temperature in February fell to 53° of frost—an unusually cold snap for the southern summer of 1914–15.

The pack ice froze into a solid mass. We were unable to free the ship and she drifted northwest, 1,000 miles during the summer, autumn, and winter. The *Endurance* was crushed, and sank in 69° S.

Our party of twenty-eight—eleven scientists and seventeen seamen—camped on the floes in lightweight tents through which the sun and moon shone and the blizzards chilled us. Our main food supply consisted of seals and penguins. So the ice, with its human freight, crept northwards—600 miles in five months.

On April 9, 1916, the floes broke up beneath our feet. The northern front of the pack was being smashed by the autumn gales of the Southern Ocean.

We launched the three boats which, by desperate efforts, we had saved from the wreck of the *Endurance,* and, by unremitting care, had preserved intact to now save our lives from crashing ice and furious gales.

Apart from ice and stormy weather, our deadliest foes at the edge of the ice were killer whales. These brutes grow to a length of over twenty-five feet and have a mouth with a four-foot stretch and teeth "according." It has been recorded that one, after being harpooned and cut up, contained twelve seals and ten porpoises! It need hardly be said that we gave thin ice a wide berth when killers were about. They will attack a blue whale which may weigh a hundred tons. While two killers seize the great whale by the lower jaw and, bearing down, force the mouth open, two others plunge in and tear out the tongue, weighing perhaps two tons. The pack of killers devour this delicacy, leaving their unfortunate victim to a slow death.

Our position then, in mid-autumn, was 60 miles southeast of Elephant Island. This desolate ice-bound island is one of the South Shetland group and lies 480 sea miles southeast of Cape Horn. It is 25 miles long east and west, and 15 miles north and south.

Ever since the loss of the *Endurance* we had known that sooner or later, when we reached the edge of the pack, we must make an ocean passage in the boats to save ourselves. Months before I had worked out courses and distances to various islands of the Southern Ocean, and even to old Cape Horn himself—blast him! Wherever we broke out of the ice we knew it would be a stormy passage of hard gales, high seas, and icy weather.

The dimensions, names, and crews of our three boats to which, under Shackleton's leadership, we were entrusting ourselves, were as follows:

The *James Caird,* built to my orders in Poplar, London, was 22 feet 6 inches long, with a 6-foot beam. I had worked out the maximum load which she could safely carry as 3 3/4 tons. She had been raised, until her depth was 3 feet 7 inches, and decked at both ends by our carpenter, which made her safer than the two smaller boats. Her captain was Sir Ernest, her crew were Wild, Vincent, Macarty, Hurley, Clark, McNeish, James, Wordie, Hussey, and Green.

The *Dudley Docker,* built in Sandefjord, Norway (22 feet long, with a beam of 6 feet and a depth of 3 feet), was the fastest of the three boats. Captain—Worsley; crew—Greenstreet, Cheetham, Macklin, McLeod, Marston, Kerr, Lees, and Holness. Her safe load was 1 1/2 tons.

The *Stancomb Wills,* built in Sandefjord, was 20 feet 8 inches long, 5 feet 6 inches beam. She was 27 1/2 inches deep from inside of her keel to the top of her gunwale. Her safe load was 1 1/4 tons. Captain—Hudson; crew—Crean, How, Bakewell, McIlroy, Blackborrow, and Stephenson.

In practice we found that we were compelled to slightly reduce the loads of the boats to lessen the amount of water shipped in heavy gales. Had our men

37

been soaked *all* the time in that bitter cold some would have died. The boats were named by Shackleton after his principal financial supporters.

Quoting from my log:

"April 9, Sunday, 1916. Position 61°56'S, 53°56'W. Moderate southwest to southeast breezes, overcast stratus and cumulo stratus. It is to be hoped the southeast breeze will hold and so save us from drifting east of Clarence." (Clarence Island lay twelve miles east of Elephant Island. If we drove past these islands, out to the open sea, it would have meant the end for twenty-eight men crowded in small boats.)

"At 7 A.M. lanes of water and leads were seen on the western horizon, with loose ice but not yet workable for boats, as a long swell running from northwest was bumping the floes together. In any case we could not have forced the boats through the brash ice between the floes. We packed everything ready for launching and struck the tents. After breakfast the ice closed a little. 11 A.M. Our floe cracked across the camp and through the site of Shackleton's tent, just vacated. Lunch at noon. 1 P.M. The pack at last opened enough to launch the boats, taking sledging stores, tents and seal blubber for fuel and food. By 1:30 we had launched, loaded, and pulled clear into an area of partially open water. Shackleton had one sledge across the stern of the *James Caird,* and the *Dudley Docker* towed another. We found it impossible to manoeuvre through heavy ice with such hindrances and were forced to abandon the sledges. 2 P.M. Having made one mile on our way we were nearly caught by a heavy rush of pack ice that drove towards us at three miles an hour. Two dangerous walls were converging as well as overtaking us, with a wave of foaming water in front. We only just managed by pulling our damnedest for an hour to save ourselves and the boats from being nipped and crushed. It was a hot hour in spite of the freezing temperature.

"Sir Ernest has cut our meals down to seal meat and blubber only, with seven ounces of dried milk per day for the party.

"Six-fifteen. Getting dark. Have rowed seven miles northwest. Forced to stop and camp owing to danger in the darkness of the boats getting crushed by the crowding floes. Just then a long floe barred our course, so we hauled up on to it. There was the added inducement of plentiful food—a crabeater seal was there before us. It was soon killed and cut up. As we hauled up the boats, secured them and the stores and pitched the tents, Green, aided by How, cooked the best cuts!"

The "galley," as we loftily called the stove that he used, had been made by Hurley from the five-gallon ash bucket of the *Endurance*. A metal cup in the base held methylated spirit which fired sliced blubber in a small pan above. This volatilized and fired big chunks of blubber in the top pan. This attained a fierce heat, above which food was cooked in a three-gallon pot resting on two iron bars. Milk made from True milk powder was boiled in the big aluminium pot of the Nanseni cooker. Three iron supports kept the galley off the snow, and a funnel at one side guided the smoke and oily blobs of soot away from our precious food.

The Cook

Our sooty-faced cook was a marvel. It seemed like a miracle when he prepared a splendid hot meal of hoosh or seal meat with tea or hot milk in thirty-five minutes from lighting the blubber fire. His only shelter from a blizzard was a piece of canvas stretched round four oars stuck upright in the snow. Clouds of oily black soot poured from the funnel. Small wonder that the cook's face was sooty, but his cheerful grin never deserted him.

The seamen, recognizing a good man, did not exercise their time-honoured right of growling at the cook. They dared not, anyway, for Sir Ernest was the cook's protector. He would not have guarded an inefficient man. Sir Ernest always set great store on the best food and cooking possible for his men. Owing to this constant care, none of the men under him ever suffered from scurvy.

Green's nickname was "Doughballs"—a fanciful name bestowed by the seamen to account for his high-pitched voice. Greenstreet, First Officer of the *Endurance,* once asked me in a stage whisper, "D'ye think he's had his pockets picked?" This query was in the nature of a libel.

Watches were set, and by 8 P.M. all, except the two lookouts, were in their sleeping bags.

The nor'west swell rolled our ice floe to and fro, rocking us gently to sleep. Slowly the floe swung round until it was end on to the swell. The watchmen, discussing the respective merits of seal brains and livers, ignored this challenge of the swell. At 11 P.M. a larger undulation rolled beneath, lifting the floe and cracking it across under the seamen's tent. We heard

40

a shout, and rushing out found their tent was tearing in halves—one half on our side and half on the other side of the crack.

In spite of the darkness, Sir Ernest, by some instinct, knew the right spot to go to. He found Holness—like a full-grown Moses—in his bag in the sea. Sir Ernest leaned over, seized the bag and, with one mighty effort, hove man and bag up on to the ice. Next second the halves of the floe swung together in the hollow of the swell with a thousand-ton blow.

It was lucky for our seaman that Sir Ernest was powerful enough to hoist the dead weight of a man and his sleeping bag, half-full of water, on to the floe. It must have been a sudden shock to wake up floating in the sea and wet to the waist. However, the rescued one soon recovered his nerve. As the camp was simmering down, after the alarm, McIlroy bumped into him rummaging in his sleeping bag and murmuring, "Lost my bloody tin of baccy." Said Micky, "You might have thanked the Boss for saving your life." "Yes, but that doesn't bring back the tobacco," replied the bereaved seaman. This incident gives an idea of the value our men set on their fast diminishing supply. The swell again separated the two halves of the floe. We suddenly realized that Sir Ernest, his tent mates and the *Caird* were on the other side.

We rushed the boat, No. 1 tent, and its inmates to safety across the crack. Sir Ernest, being last, could not hold on to the boat and got left behind in the darkness. At Wild's shout we hove the *Wills* into the sea and joyfully ferried our marooned leader back to his men. Our movements were hastened by hearing a killer whale blow right alongside us.

"No more sleep. Killers were blowing all round. All hands kept warm by tramping the floe and huddling round the blazing fire of seal blubber till dawn.

"Every two hours we cooked more seal meat and had another meal."

To prevent boredom Micky told us how to make eleven varieties of cocktails with scandalous names for each. He also sang songs and told tales hot enough to keep the cold out. To crown all, Bob Clark made a joke —I think it was about the killers blowing us up. We amused ourselves so well till dawn that, in spite of $24°$ of frost, we almost imagined we were at a picnic.

"This day we have seen five Cape pigeons (from the open sea), three paddys, three fulmars, ten Adelie penguins, sixteen Antarctic petrels, hundreds of snow petrels, many whales and crabeaters."

In spite of our troubles and losing sleep the whole party was in good spirits, for, at last, we had exchanged inaction for action. We had been waiting and drifting at the mercy of the pack ice. There had been nothing that we could do to escape. Now there were more dangers and hardships, but we were working and struggling to save ourselves. We were full of hope and optimism—feelings that Shackleton always fostered.

"Tenth, Monday. Strong easterly breeze; overcast, misty with snow squalls. 5:30 A.M. Hoosh—very welcome after our night walk on the floe. The pack ice had closed round our floe, but at 8:10 we managed to launch the boats, load them and proceed at first with oars. Later as the ice became looser, we set sail. 11 A.M. Struck open water for six miles. As we sailed, spray flew over the boats and froze on the men and the stores. We rounded the north end of the pack, but found that in the open the sea was too heavy for our deeply laden boats. Besides the weight of twenty-eight men, we had three tents, spare clothing, our sleeping bags, 'Primus' lamps and paraffin, oars, masts, sails, and three weeks' food for the party.

"After conferring with Wild and me, Sir Ernest decided we must rely on getting enough seals and penguins for our main supply. He ordered that one-third of our food must be abandoned, leaving us with only two weeks' supply.

"We returned to the shelter of the pack, unloaded, and hauled the boats up on a floeberg at 3:30 P.M. There we abandoned one week's supply of food. While we pitched the tents and secured the boats, Green raided the abandoned stores. Presently he produced the best and largest meal we had eaten for five months.

"By my reckoning we made ten miles northwest today. I also hoped that the strong easterly breeze that had been blowing would set up a fair current. To make up for last night's lost sleep we turned in at 8 P.M., the lookouts keeping a watch of one hour each."

Our floeberg was ninety feet long, and the highest part of it was twenty feet above the sea. We had a glorious sleep for twelve hours, but through the night the northwest swell increased to a great height. The surrounding floes were hurled by the swell against our home, undermining it so that large pieces continuously broke off.

"Eleventh, Tuesday. When we turned out we found

that we had lost nearly half of our floeberg. Strong northeast breeze, overcast and misty. Cold weather, 20° of frost.''

The swell had increased to a tremendous height and the pack had closed in around us. It was as magnificent and beautiful a sight as I have ever seen. Great rolling hills of jostling ice sweeping past us in half-mile-long waves. A few dark lines and cracks sharply contrasted against the white pack were the only signs of the sea beneath. But it was a sight we did not like, for the floes were thudding against our floeberg with increasing violence. Our temporary home was being swept away at an unpleasantly rapid rate. We saw that in a few hours our foothold would be cut from under us. We and the boats would be thrown into that seething mass of heaving floes. There would have been no hope for us. It was an anxious time. Shackleton, Wild and I went to the highest point so frequently to look north for open water that one or more of us were on the lookout there all the time. Before lunch we had made a track to the summit that looked as though a regiment had passed there.

The undermined banks broke away at such a rate that twice we had to draw the boats back into safety.

After what seemed an eternity we saw a dark line—open water—to the north slowly drawing nearer. It became a race between the rescuing open sea and the collapse of our foothold.

Our floeberg was about eighty feet deep in the sea, so that its base, fortunately for us, was caught by a different current. This carried it towards the dark band of welcome sea.

Just in time—two hours after noon—we reached a narrow arm of open water. As the pack edged away from us the floeberg rolled and almost dipped one side into the sea. With a rush we slid the boats down the six-foot cliff into the water.

The *James Caird* caught on a ledge of ice, but her crew smartly pushed her off and saved her from capsizing. We hurled the stores in without stowing and, leaping on them, pushed and poled the boats out into safety. It was a narrow enough escape.

Dodging in and out through loose patches of pack, we sailed two miles west into more open sea. Then the *Stancomb Wills* fell astern and got into trouble. It was blowing half a gale from northeast, and it looked as though the *Wills* would be jammed on a lee shore—the front of the main pack.

My boat being the fastest, Shackleton sent me back to tow the *Wills* clear. It was sunset by the time we overhauled and rejoined Shackleton.

We continued to sail west until we saw a floe large enough to promise some shelter for the night. At dusk we made fast in its lee.

As we tended the boats and ate cold rations, Green and How landed the galley and boiled the milk. While this operation was proceeding some of our irrepressibles were making impatient calf noises to amuse Green, until we were all handed mugs of glorious hot milk. The galley was then embarked.

Suddenly masses of ice eddied round the floe, threatening to hole the boats. We cast off hurriedly. During the night we dodged from one patch of ice to another, but could get no shelter.

"A cold, wet, rotten night—all hands wet and shivering—with rain at first and snow showers. One oilskin only in the *Docker*. No sleep. After midnight the temperature fell to 25° of frost, and we could not get enough rowing to keep us warm. I wanted to pull slowly to the west all night for the sake of progress and to keep the men warm, but Sir Ernest would not agree. He feared the danger of holing the boats against the ice and the difficulty of keeping them together in the dark. At dawn we set sail and steered west-southwest on the starboard tack. This twenty-four hours we have seen numerous fulmars, snow petrels, silver petrels, giant petrels (almost as big as albatrosses), stormy petrels, and Antarctic petrels. Hundreds of crabeaters in all directions on the pack and many whales.

"April 12. 62°15'S, 53°07'W. Strong northwest breeze. Cloudy and misty, with sleet showers. The temperature during the last three days has been going up and down—mostly down—but we had no thermometer in the *Docker*."

When our crop of minor frostbites increased, we hailed Hussey in the *Caird*. "What's the temperature, meteorologist?" Our youthful humorist invariably gave the information wrapped up in comic abuse. This was received politely if the temperature was reasonably cold, but if it was below zero he got a hot reply. The northwest wind brought the temperature nearly up to freezing point, but no pleasure to us. It turned the snow to sleet and rain, which froze on men and stores, making us wet, cold, and miserable. Fortunately our previous experiences had so toughened us that we managed to weather it out.

46

After breakfast, as soon as the horizon cleared, I took observations for longitude with the sextant. At noon I observed the latitude.

When I worked out the position, it was a terrible disappointment. I had previously told Shackleton that I thought we had made thirty miles towards Elephant Island. The sights proved we were thirty miles farther away and had been driven nineteen miles farther south. Shackleton ran the *James Caird* down to us and asked, "What have we made, Skipper?" "Thirty miles astern, sir,' I muttered. It was so bad that he did not tell the men. He merely said, "We haven't done as well as we expected." Even so I got a black look or two.

In retrospect, the childlike mentality of many of the party, in respect to our progress, had its humorous side. On the pack ice, which was outside any human control, they seemed to hold me responsible for the drift. At noon, when I worked out where the ice had carried our camp, I was asked, "What have we done?" If I replied "Four miles north,' it was 'Well done, Skipper, have a cigarette." If I said "Fourteen miles north," I became the hero of the day. Cigarettes, bits of bannocks and lumps of chocolate were offered to me. On the other hand, if we drifted eight miles south, I received black looks and was avoided like a pestilence. Like the Ancient Mariner, "Instead of the cross the albatross about my neck they hung." Few besides Shackleton sympathized with me.

This last setback came when it was imperative to make speed to the land. A strong head current had poured out from the Bransfield Strait, which lay ninety miles west of us.

The current had been speeded up by the heavy northwest gale which we knew, by the swell, had been blowing off Cape Horn. Our advance had been completely reversed and we had been carried south into the pack again.

Though the responsibility must rest on the leader of an expedition, I can never forget my acute anxiety for the next two days. If there was a mistake in my sights, which were taken under very difficult conditions, twenty-eight men would have sailed out to death. Fortunately the sights proved correct. We made the island ahead fifty hours later.

Shortly after noon we suddenly ran out of the main pack into open sea, with bergs and small islands of pack scattered about. There was a long swell from the open sea, and we flattered ourselves we were going to make a good passage either to the island or else to Graham Land, the northern extreme of the Antarctic Continent.

We sailed past a strange berg that resembled a pig-faced prehistoric monster. It rolled slowly to the swell. For five minutes at a time the grotesque face rolled down 100 feet into the sea. A long pause and it slowly rolled up again, the water pouring in torrents down the monster's face. It seemed to us to be weeping tears of rage at our escape from the pack.

"In the evening we saw enormous 'woolpacks' of cumulus to northwest—the aftermath of the gale which had raised the great swell. They were breaking up. These great cumulus are seldom or never seen over pack ice. The sea appeared open to southwest, and the heaviest pack lay behind us to the east.

"From here onward, to the departure of the *James Caird* from Elephant Island, was written from memory nine months later, as I was too busy to do so in the boat, what with steering, navigating with frostbitten fingers, etc. etc."

The sea was clear to southwest, and the wind having increased and hauled northwest was ahead for the island. Sir Ernest discussed with Wild and me the advantages of making for Hope Bay in the north of Graham Land, and decided that was the best course under the circumstances.

We sailed west-southwest into the dusk, but later met long streams of ice that we could not weather. To avoid being caught between the streams in the dark, we made fast to the largest floe we could find. Unfortunately it was not large enough to give us much shelter from the rising gale. The sea was too rough for the cook to land his galley, so we boiled milk over a "Primus" in each boat.

We made a practice of eating our food and swallowing our milk at far greater heat than normal men could have borne. So we gave our chilled bodies warmth enough to keep us alive against cold, fatigue, and lack of sleep.

The painters of the *Caird* and the *Docker* were made fast on the floe, and the *Wills* moored between us. The three boats lay side by side during supper. Later the seas running round the floe bumped and chafed the boats, so that we had to slack the other two astern of us.

As the last of our supper was vanishing at its usual amazing rate, the wind suddenly shifted to southeast.

The boats drove broadside on to the jagged edge of the floe. To save them being stove in, we hurriedly cut our painter, losing valuable rope, and pushed off.

All that night in the open sea we "bothered" about —as our seamen did *not* say. The *James Caird* made fast astern of us and the *Stancomb Wills* astern of her. Most of the time we pulled ahead, towing the two boats to prevent them bumping. We had the best of it—the exercise kept us from freezing, and also kept us awake. I am keen on rowing and enjoyed my spells at the oars. Some were not usually keen on rowing, but all preferred it, that night, to the shivering spells between.

The temperature suddenly fell to 36° of frost. It was so cold that our Burberry overalls crackled and ice and frost fell off us as we rowed. When the moon came out, we saw that beards were white with frost, moustaches knobbed with ice, and each man's breath formed clouds of vapour, showing white against his grubby face.

Snow showers swept up from southeast and the surface of the sea froze in spite of wind and swell. This made patches of sludgy ice into which we towed the boats for smoother water. Another compensation— the sudden change of wind that almost spoiled our supper—had given us a fair wind for Elephant Island.

So far this boat escape had been a "rake's progress." We had rowed. We had sailed. Shackleton and I had taken turns at towing the smallest boat. We had been hindered by pack ice, head winds, currents, and heavy swells. We had hauled up on the ice and escaped again. Now, after three days of toil and exposure, without sleep, we were forty miles farther from Elephant Island.

In spite of all, the men, inspired by Shackleton, were magnificent. Their courage and humour came to the front when most needed. It was well that they had been toughened and tempered to hardness for this ordeal, by the progressively severer conditions which we had undergone since leaving civilization.

Shackleton and several of us had been trained in square-rigged ships. After the cold of South Georgia our party worked the *Endurance* through 3,000 miles of pack ice—a fine, hard, open-air life. Then came 1,000 miles drift, with temperature down to 100° of frost, but in the comfort of the ship. Then 600 miles drift in gale-worn tents lying by night on snow that, melted by the heat of our bodies, ran into our sleeping bags until we lay in pools of ice-cold water. Now that conditions were worse the men, like true British seamen, ceased complaining and said, "Grin and bear it. Growl and go."

At dawn on the thirteenth, it blew strong from southeast, with clear weather. Cumulus—typical of open sea—scudded across the blue sky.

The men were bleary-eyed from exposure and want of sleep. Shackleton hailed me. I took the *Dudley Docker* alongside. After a short talk we decided to take advantage of the fair wind and steer, again, for Elephant Island. The food stores were distributed amongst the boats, so that, if they separated, no one would go short.

Sail was set, and we steered northwest. As the boats

gathered way before the fair breeze our spirits rose. We forgot our disappointments. We were making headway to the land—solid land! How fine it would be to feel good earth beneath our feet, after sixteen months spent on the accursed heaving, restless ice. We felt the exhilaration that yachtsmen feel. We were yachting though in a rather overperilous manner.

As we rolled along we chipped and scraped off the ice that had formed during the night on the bows and sterns of our three craft. We could not cook while we were sailing, so Shackleton gave permission for every man to eat as much biscuit, cold ration, nut food, and West Indies loaf sugar as he liked. This was a fairly safe order as we had found by experience that "short commons" had so contracted our stomachs that we were unable to eat too much at one time.

It was more than sixteen months since the party had been in a rough sea. Several were "off colour" for two days, but four were seasick and unable to eat. I was sorry for them. It was bad enough for frostbitten men to be huddled in deep-laden boats while seas broke over them, without having seasickness added. However, our amusement was aroused by the dismay of one who was fond of saving his food and, later, eating it in front of others who had not been so frugal. This procedure had an infuriating effect on most of the hungry onlookers. Now this man, suffering from sea-sickness, gazed impotently at us—ravening sea wolves —making the rations disappear. He got scant sympathy.

Sailing on at a fair rate we came into areas of loose pack ice, interspersed with many lumps. Taking turns, we leaned over the bows, poling the lumps away with indifferent success. Many were too heavy to be moved quickly enough. The *Caird* struck one that holed her above the water line. Soon after we saw a piece of sealskin protruding through the hole to keep the water out. After that we reefed sails to avoid more damage to the boats.

At noon we again came into an area of comparatively open water. Shackleton led in the *Caird,* followed by the *Docker* and the *Wills* in that order. Occasionally he sent me ahead to prospect, but generally his orders were for the boats to keep within thirty yards of each other.

Our sails showed dark in contrast to the patches of white pack. We looked like a fleet of exploring or marauding Vikings. Sailing on we came to large areas of freezing sea with slush and "pancakes," through which we forced the boats at much reduced speed.

Lying about in the slush and on the "pancakes" were countless thousands of dead fish, some of which were eight inches long. They had been caught and frozen by the sudden freezing of the sea. They looked like splashes and bars of silver glistening in the sun. The petrels and Cape pigeons were enjoying an unusual feast. Like the birds, we would have relished a splendid meal of fish, but we dared not waste time gathering them.

In the afternoon the temperature rose slightly, the sea thawed and became more open. We made good headway, but had to take a second reef in the sails as the boats were shipping much water and steering badly in the rising wind and sea.

At sunset I thought the wind would soon moderate, and advised Shackleton to stand on all night, but he considered it safer to heave to. This we did by means of three oars bent on to the *Docker*'s painter for a sea anchor. The other boats were made fast astern of us.

We had sailed clear of the pack ice so quickly that there had been no time to lay in a stock of ice for drinking water. All hands were suffering painfully from thirst. However, by superior cunning, we in the *Docker* had secured four precious blocks of ice. These we "whacked out," with comparative honesty, amongst the other crews. By very strict rationing we managed to make the ice last all night. It seems strange that men in such cold weather, frequently soaked by seas breaking over them, should have suffered more from thirst than hunger, but so it was. Throughout the night Shackleton was concerned with the welfare of the men. He always took great care of them, but now, owing to the incessant hardships, he was obviously anxious. At intervals he hailed us and the *Wills* to find how we were faring. The answers were always cheerful, but Marston raised a laugh by humorously shouting, "All right, but I'd like some dry mitts." There was nothing dry in the boats except our parched mouths. Shackleton replied, "I left a pair at home. You can have them if you'll drop in and tell 'em I'm coming." The humour may have been slightly heavy, but we were eager to seize on any excuse for a laugh.

The sea, breaking over the boats, froze in great masses on bows and sterns. The temperature was below zero, but we could not waste precious matches looking at the thermometer. There was no real sleep that night, though some dozed in each other's arms for warmth.

After dark the wind moderated, as I had foretold, which, however, did not prove that Shackleton's decision was wrong. But I had a twofold anxiety. One was that delay might give time for a heavy gale to rise. The other was about the men. Some were becoming exhausted with fatigue, intense cold, and lack of sleep for three days and nights. We knew there was more to follow. Next night the delay ran us into a gale so furious that it was providential neither of the smaller boats foundered.

At daybreak on the fourteenth there was a gentle southwest breeze and clear weather. A magnificent and gorgeously beautiful sunrise raised our spirits, but not our hopes. It was a high dawn presaging a gale.

It had been impossible to sleep in the two open boats. In the *Docker* we laid our flimsy tent on the ice-clad boxes of stores. Pulling its folds over us, we compressed ourselves into a shivering mass of humanity. We were like those monkeys which, during a cold night in the forest, lock themselves into a ball for mutual warmth. If one gets left out and, pushing in, disturbs the others, a furious row ensues. So it was with us. When some shivering unfortunate on the outside tried to push in, there instantly arose a frightful burst of profanity and dire threats of vengeance from the disturbed men.

Greenstreet and I bore this till some time after midnight. We then crawled out, swung our arms, stamped our feet, punched each other, and occasionally solaced

55

ourselves by smoking. We used four valuable matches.

When daylight came we stood looking for some minutes at the writhing mass of suffering men clearly outlined under the tent. It shook and heaved up and down. It trembled and wriggled. Ever and again, at some fresh convulsion, it emitted terrible oaths profaning the morning air. Suddenly we could stand it no longer. We burst into such yells of laughter that we roused the crews of the other boats as well as our own. We were possibly a bit overwrought, but even now, years after, I laugh whenever I recall that scene.

In the growing light we cleared the boats of the heavy accumulations of ice that were weighing them down. Before we could ship the rudder we had to chip and scrape all ice off the stern and clear the gudgeon holes before we could get the pintles in.

After this we ranged alongside the *Caird* and tacked a square of sealskin over the hole in her bows. A good temporary patch that would keep the water out in a high sea. The next job was to haul in the painter and recover the oars which we had been using as an improvised sea anchor. When we reached the oars we found each encased in ice to the thickness of a man's thigh. We had to chip them clear before we could lift them aboard. Setting sail, we stood north, and again all hands were cheered by our progress.

For breakfast we had cold rations. There were a few very small lumps of ice remaining. These we sucked slowly. When they were finished we became so terribly thirsty that we were unable to eat. We then resorted to chewing pieces of raw bloody seal meat.

This stayed our thirst as well as our ravenous hun-

56

ger for a while, but later we were more parched than before. Probably this was due to salts in the seal's blood.

In the *Wills* Blackborrow's feet were badly frostbitten. Nothing could be done then except that Dr. McIlroy occasionally massaged the sufferer's feet. Blackborrow, the youngest of the party, was twenty years old. That may have accounted for the fact that he was the only one to suffer permanently from frostbite. Shackleton and the other six Antarctic veterans had come through well, but equally so had Greenstreet, the two doctors, Clark, Wordie, and I. Most of us had suffered no more than frostbitten fingers which all were liable to. The only notice we took of a frostbitten finger was to remove our sodden mitts and massage the finger until it recovered.

Shackleton said to me, later, "All the time I was attending to the boats and watching the condition of the men, Wild sat calmly steering the *Caird.* He never batted an eyelid. Always the same confident, blue-eyed little man, unmoved by cold or fatigue. He was a tower of strength, as I knew he would be."

This was only what we all expected of that grand veteran of the Antarctic, but it was typical of Shackleton to praise his friend so generously.

As the daylight strengthened, we saw to northeast the lofty snow-clad peak of Clarence Island tipped with pink against the sunrise. A little later the peaks and ice uplands of Elephant Island showed cold and gloomy, thirty-five miles to the north-northwest. They were both exactly on the bearings I had laid off. Shackleton, always generous with praise, congratulated me on the accuracy of my navigation under difficult conditions, after two days of dead reckoning working in and out amongst floes with no accurate means of checking compass courses and two nights drifting at the mercy of winds and currents.

I took my honours unblushingly, but to tell the truth there had been a large element of luck in making this good landfall. I had been very anxious, for our lives depended on reaching land speedily. My worries departed; the men forgot thirst, hunger, and fatigue. All cheered up visibly in spite of the forbidding look of our goal.

The sea had gone down, and the gentle westerly breeze on our port beam filling our sails, we made steady headway towards our Promised Land. But not fast enough—out came the oars and all day we rowed hard to the north. The exercise increased our thirst but warmed us. Our hands melted our mitts and gradually melted the ice off the oar looms. We could work the oars without constantly letting them slip from our grasp. I cannot remember all the names the oars were called before this happened, but they certainly did not lack variety nor pungency. At noon the temperature rose to $22°$. Our hard work taken in turns made the weather seem warm.

I had not slept for eighty hours. This seemed strange for one whose capacity for sleep and food was a byword, but we were all held up in some mysterious way by the urgency of affairs. In the afternoon I had been steering for nine hours while leading the other boats and found it almost impossible to keep awake. Greenstreet—a fine seaman—continually urged me to hand over the tiller and have a nap. I had, however, become so obsessed with steering for the island and maintaining the utmost speed that I kept on when I should have handed over to him. The consequence was that at intervals I fell asleep for a few seconds and the *Docker,* with the *Wills* in tow, sheered off her course. Everyone through fatigue and loss of sleep had slightly lost his judgment. The first time I swung the two boats off to starboard Shackleton, following in the *Caird,* thought I was making off for Clarence Island against his decision to land on Elephant Island. The next time he was convinced of this, not realizing that I was momentarily falling asleep as I steered. He naturally became indignant. The third time I happened to steer to port. This puzzled and annoyed him so much that he shouted, "Are you trying to do the dirty on me?" He would never normally have made such a remark. It angered those of my crew who heard it, and annoyed me, through my haze of sleep, that my efforts were misunderstood. I was so upset that I started to reply in kind, but suddenly realizing that he must be in a similar state, plus his terrible anxiety and responsibility, merely waved my arm in deprecation of argument. I was quite awake afterwards.

I mention this incident to show how fatigue was beginning to tell. When later Shackleton found out the cause of my erratic steering he made amends in his customary handsome fashion.

Before sunset the wind hauled ahead. It was "Down sails and pull" towards the south point of the island. We in the *Docker,* being fastest in moderate weather, then towed the *Caird* and the *Wills* in turn. Their crews continued to row hard to ease the strain on us.

After dark the head wind increased to a gale against which we could make no headway with the oars. Up went our sails again to beat to windward and into shelter. We continued to tow the *Wills.* Then, as the gale increased, the larger size of the *Caird* and her deck cover enabling her to carry more sail put her in the lead. Finally I had to hand my tow over to Shackleton. For two hours after this we kept side by side—an exciting race in the gale. So close were we that we repeatedly hailed each other, more for company than information because our words were mostly unintelligible, being swept away by the gale.

Steadily the wind increased, and the sea became so heavy that we had to head up into the wind to keep our boat from floundering. It must be remembered that our freeboard was 1 foot 8 inches. That means that our gunwale was only 20 inches above the sea in smooth water. At the same time Shackleton had to handle the *Caird* very carefully to keep the *Wills* afloat as she towed behind. The depth of the *Stancomb Wills,* as previously recorded, was 27 1/2 inches. Her freeboard was only 17 inches. It looked dangerously small for an open boat. The *Docker* went well to windward, but the *Caird* drew slightly ahead on our lee bow.

There is a big bay seventeen miles broad and twelve to fourteen miles deep on the southeast side of Elephant Island. Approaching in the blackness of the gale and thick snow squalls, we could see no sign of this or the land, but we knew that if we came very close in to the weather shore, we would be warned by a decrease of the heavy sea. The gale was howling from northwest bitterly cold off the great ice sheet of Elephant Island. I edged the *Docker* still more to windward hoping to reach smoother water in the bay and also to avoid being driven over to Clarence Island.

We were in the midst of confused lumpy seas which, running round the island from two directions, were far more dangerous for small boats than the straight-running waves of a heavy gale in open sea. It was impossible to dodge every sea and, at intervals, I shipped a heavy one. Then it was "Bale! Bale like hell!"

Fortunately, at some time before midnight, the gale hauled to southwest, enabling us to make inshore. We could not say when the change came because our compass was smashed and we dared not risk many matches in trying to look at my pocket compass.

When I felt that the wind had shifted, I kept the boat away from the wind for five or six minutes and ran down close to the *Caird.* I shouted, "I'd better make inshore, Boss, and look for a landing." He answered, "All right, but don't lose sight of us." I luffed to windward, but as the boats drew clear a thick snow squall came down which lasted for an hour. When it cleared we could see nothing of the others, which made us anxious for their safety. It was now sometime in the very early hours of the fifteenth.

Squall by squall the wind grew fiercer and the sea heavier. Through a rift in the clouds the moon shone out on the stormy sea and for two minutes revealed the ghostly white uplands and glaciers of the island. Another squall blotted everything out. We heard whales blow right alongside. They may have been killers, but, whatever they were, a push from one of them would have capsized us. If they were killers we would have had a quicker end. Soon to our great relief they left us for some nobler quarry than dirty, smelly little men in Burberry overalls.

Suddenly a light shone out to leeward. A joyful sight. Shackleton was shining his compass light on the *Caird*'s sails as a guide to us. Somehow we lit our candle under the cloth of the tent hoping that the light would shine through to reassure Sir Ernest. He told me next day that he saw nothing of our dim light. With that candle our poor fellows lit their pipes—our only solace—for our raging thirst prevented us from eating. At the same time we got a glimpse of my compass which showed us how we were heading and that the wind was fair.

As Shackleton's light disappeared, we found ourselves in a dangerous tide rip which, combined with the steep, heavy sea, constituted a very great danger. The seas leapt simultaneously over bows, beam, and stern. Everyone baled furiously, and Lees, who admitted he was a rotten seaman, distinguished himself by strenuous baling, Greenstreet, scooping out water, straightened up for three instants and said, "Look, the Major's putting out more than we've shipped." It was even so; the poor fellow was gamely baling and vomiting at the same time. Baling furiously the crew moved the sea to the right side—the outside of the brave little *Dudley Docker.*

The danger was so great that we could not keep the boat away from the wind to rejoin Shackleton. We could only pray that the *Wills,* the smallest boat, still floated. Greenstreet was splendid, never losing hope

62

and always ready to crack some appalling sailor-joke. I had previously ordered some of the least vital of the stores to be placed handy for throwing overboard. At the worst time, when it was almost impossible to keep the boat afloat, I said, "Dump those stores." Greenstreet replied, "I'd wait; she'll come through." I countermanded the order and, after an hour, was glad I took his advice. He and Dr. Macklin were my bower anchors that night and as stroke oars when we rowed on that passage. Those "old-timers" of the Antarctic, Cheetham and McLeod, pulled their weight. Mac was a typical deep-sea shellback and "growl." The merchant seaman's saying, "Growl an' go," must have been his motto, in spite of which he was a great favourite. Cheetham was a pirate to the tips of his frostbitten fingers. He specialized in match plunder. Matches, always valuable, became, during the drift on the ice, communal property.

In the height of this gale Cheetham's pipe naturally went out. As I steered I felt someone snuggle up to me. Then I heard Cheetham, who knew I was economical, whisper, "Can you give me a match, sir?" I gave him one, but the other men were annoyed, so that later, when a sea had again extinguished his pipe and he tried to cadge another match, I put him off. His voice then grew so pathetic that I had not the heart to deny him the pleasure of a smoke. I said, "I'll sell you one." "Right, sir. What price?" he inquired. "A bottle of champagne," I said with a chuckle. "Done," he replied. "As soon as I open my little pub in Hull the champagne's yours." Poor Cheetham! I don't think he ever bought "my little pub," but he never paid the debt, for he was killed fighting the Germans in the North Sea just before the Armistice.

Marston and Kerr were hard, willing workers. The former appeared to almost relish this sort of work, and stood the strain of those ninety hours as well as anyone. Greenstreet and I had been awake all that time. Later I found that neither Shackleton nor Wild had slept during four days and nights.

To our surprise we found that the deep-sea men stood the strain and exposure better than most of our North Sea fishermen. Dr. McIlroy was another surprise. He was slim and dark and joined the expedition fresh from practising in Malaya, but came through the cold in perfect condition.

The repeated soakings in bitter cold, with thirst, hunger and fatigue, caused numerous minor frostbites. At about 3 A.M. Greenstreet managed to sleep for half an hour, and then found his right foot was badly frostbitten. Lees partly cured it by removing boot and socks and massaging the foot. He then heroically held Greenstreet's bare foot against his stomach under his sweater!

About this time the weather again grew thick with snow and spindrift. We knew we were closer to the land, but could not see it. Constant peering to windward to ease her into the heaviest seas, and the continuous dash of salt water into my face had almost bunged up my eyes. I could not see nor judge properly, and sometimes fell asleep at the tiller for one or two vital seconds. Greenstreet again urged me to hand over the tiller.

Between 3 and 4 A.M. he found that I was cramped

Entering the pack ice of
the Weddell Sea, December, 1914
(Scott Polar Research Institute).

65

The wake of the *Endurance*
(National Library of Australia).

The *Endurance* under sail
(National Library of Australia).

67

New leads in the pack ice covered with "ice flowers"
(Scott Polar Research Institute).

How the pack ice breaks up under pressure
(Scott Polar Research Institute).

Deck of the *Endurance* after a snowfall
(Scott Polar Research Institute).

Endeavoring to cut the ship out of the ice
(Scott Polar Research Institute).

Caught fast in the ice
(Scott Polar Research Institute).

A dog team in very rough ice conditions
(Scott Polar Research Institute).

A great castellated berg that menaced the ship.
Note figures at left. (Scott Polar Research Institute).

71

Photographer Hurley at work (Scott Polar Research Institute).

Frank Wild with dog team leader (National Library of Australia).

Heavy blocks of ice rafted up and tilted by the pressure (Scott Polar Research Institute).

Clark in the biological laboratory aboard the *Endurance* (Scott Polar Research Institute).

Midwinter, 1915 (Scott Polar Research Institute).

The *Endurance* battling blocks of pressure ice
(National Library of Australia).

Overleaf: A night photograph of the *Endurance*
(Scott Polar Research Institute).

75

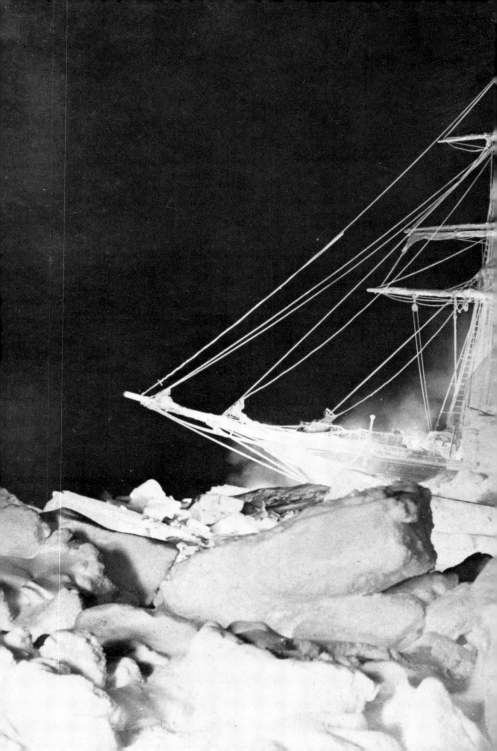

The *Endurance* caught in a pressure crack, shortly before she sank (Scott Polar Research Institute).

Overleaf: Wreckage of the *Endurance* (Scott Polar Research Institute).

Return of the sun after the long winter darkness. Note ice crystals on rigging. (Scott Polar Research Institute).

79

by wet and cold. I had been steering in a constrained position, sitting on the stores, for twenty hours. As he seized the tiller, I said, "Let me know when you close the land." As Macklin and McLeod put me under the dripping folds of the tent, I asked them to straighten me out and rub my thighs and groins. While they did this—straightening me out like opening a jackknife— I fell fast asleep in their hands. After they had vigorously massaged my stomach and legs they lay, one on each side, under the tent to keep some of the breaking seas off me.

For more than an hour I was utterly oblivious of all around. Greenstreet, steering, sighted the Island ahead at about 5 A.M. Soon after, with daylight, he found he was quickly closing the land.

Great crags thrust up through the snow. A wall of ice faced us with high seas rolling along its base. Another snow squall swept down; Greenstreet could not see which way he should steer. "Wake the Skipper," he said. Two of the men pulled me out. For three or four minutes they tried hard to waken me. They became alarmed at their failure, not realizing what a good sleep I was having. Cheetham asked Dr. Macklin if I was dead. After a brief inspection he announced that the corpse was alive! McLeon, realizing the necessity of bringing me into action, said, "I'll wake the Skipper." He did so by dealing me two good kicks on the back of the head. I sat up suddenly and said, "Keep her away four points," in response to Greenstreet's inquiry as to how he should steer.

I was told of some difficulty in rousing me. I had no idea of the drastic method adopted to do so until three years later, when we were together with Shackleton in the army in North Russia, Macklin told me how it was done.

I took the tiller again and ran her off before the gale, following the coast round to the north. We had come to the northeast end of the big bay on the south of Elephant Island. For half an hour we were beset by a new danger, caused by the change of wind to southwest four hours earlier. This brought the heavy sea right astern. As we ran before the gale these seas threatened to curl over our stern and swamp us. There was also, for a few minutes, a danger of capsizing if the sail gybed in our efforts to keep clear of the cliffs and glacier fronts close alongside. We ran parallel to these cliffs for twenty minutes; then, clearing the big bay, we rounded a point into comparatively smooth water. The heavy sea was cut off by the land and the gale decreased. We revelled in our safety. In the lee of the island the sky cleared and the sun came out.

Our spirits rose as we sailed on while small lumps of glacier ice tinkled against our bows. I steered in, till we were twenty yards offshore, to secure some lumps of fresh-water ice. The men leaned over and caught a number of chunks to the tune of cracked laughter. Chipping the salt off the ice with their knives, the men joyfully sucked until, parched tongues and mouths being moistened, they remembered their hunger. When Greenstreet scraped a chunk and handed it to me, I thought gratefully what a hell of a fine fellow he was. What a glorious sensation it was to feel fresh water trickling down my burning throat.

Then we ate. We chewed biscuits, nut food, pemmican, and raw seal meat. A queer mixture, but we could have eaten leather. We were happy knowing that we would soon find a resting place.

Suddenly we were assailed with fears for our companions with Shackleton. The last we had seen of them was the light shining on their sails. In particular I feared for the *Wills*. I looked anxiously ahead and to seaward.

Our own position was still difficult. The men were nearly exhausted. We coasted past high cliffs and glacier fronts for fourteen miles without one possible landing place.

Then I saw a low rocky beach that promised an escape from the sea. For a moment we were amazed by the sight of two small masts. Then we realized that they belonged to our boats and our amazement changed to joy. They were making into the landing just ahead of us. We gave them three cheers. We landed twenty minutes later. At 10 A.M. there was a happy reunion. But there was little time for congratulations. It took us until three in the afternoon to get through our work.

While some carried the stores ashore others hauled the boats out of the water and across the rocky ledges. Green soon converted a sea elephant, that we killed, into glorious hot hoosh. He followed it up with hot milk. While we continued the work Green and his assistant had a good meal themselves. Then they took a deep breath and leisurely cooked us another meal.

Some of our men were almost lightheaded as well as lighthearted. When they landed they reeled about, laughing uproariously. Others sat on the shingle and, like harmless lunatics, let it run through their hands to reassure themselves that they really were on dry land at last. Blackborrow was unable to walk on his frostbitten feet. Everyone had red-rimmed eyes. Shackleton was bowed down and aged by the ordeal, accentuated by the responsibility and strain of holding the boats together and keeping his men alive.

As soon as we had placed the stores and boats above high-water mark, we pitched the tents and laid out our sodden sleeping-bags, which partially dried in the wind and sun.

Shackleton, Wild, Hurley, and I then inspected our beach. It was not a reassuring inspection. The beach was four feet above ordinary high-water mark. Inaccessible cliffs rose sheer behind, and the first easterly gale would have swept us from our hard-won foothold. We had camped at Cape Valentine—the northeast corner of Elephant Island.

We crept into our sleeping bags. Their smell did not offend us. They seemed heavenly to us. There were sharp stones beneath our shoulders, but they did not worry us. We were only too glad to feel solid land beneath us after our nightmare passage and after living precariously for six months on heaving ice. I think that most of us, before falling asleep, uttered a little prayer of thankfulness for our escape.

During one hundred hours of hardship and exposure Shackleton and Wild had not slept. Greenstreet and I had each slept for about an hour. It was not surprising, therefore, that now we could sleep safely, we slumbered happily for eighteen hours. It would have been nineteen, but for the hour that each of us who were fit spent in keeping a watch on the camp and a careful scrutiny of the weather. If the wind had shifted to east we would have launched the boats before the sea rose and sailed west for a safer camp.

All night the blubber fire blazed. Each watchman cooked and ate seal liver, brains, and steak. After the enforced abstinence from food and drink we took a gluttonous delight in sizzling seal meat and hot tea or milk.

At 11 A.M. on the sixteenth the camp came to life. The day was spent in feasting, drying clothes and sleeping bags, and overhauling gear. Our beach resembled a dirty and exceedingly disreputable gipsy encampment.

While we were so employed Wild took the *Stancomb Wills,* lightly laden, to the westward to look for a safer camp. At 8 P.M., guided by our blubber fire, he returned with a report of a safer landing seven or eight miles west. There was no possible landing between. This proved that, including the fourteen miles of coast skirted by us in the *Docker,* there was only one landing place in twenty-two miles of coast. Neither our landing nor Wild's could be used with winds between northwest and east. For that and climatic reasons our men pronounced Elephant Island with the "t" silent, and an "h" prefixed.

On the seventeenth pack ice appeared to the east. It was drifting rapidly towards our beach. There was danger that it might pile around our landing and imprison us. It was high time to leave our precarious foothold. But several of the men seemed doubtful of committing themselves to the dangers of another boat journey, however short. A few seemed to shudder mentally at the memory of their ordeal. Several had not quite recovered their strength, so the work of hauling the boats across the beach and rocky ledges occupied us till 10 A.M. By the time we had launched and loaded the boats, embarked the party, and pulled clear of the shore, another hour had elapsed. In moving the boats we had met with misfortune. Using the oars for rollers, three had been broken in the process. This proved to be a very serious loss.

From the camp we were leaving at Cape Valentine the coast ran in an irregular line eight miles west to our next camp. We hoped that by pulling steadily we should arrive there early in the afternoon. But events turned out differently.

A northerly swell was thundering against the cliffs near the landing. We rowed west along the north shore of the island in a calm for ten minutes. Ten minutes later we were struggling against a "southerly buster." In another ten minutes it was blowing a heavy gale from south-southwest, but by dint of hard pulling we succeeded in drawing close under a great cliff that gave us shelter. Even there back squalls and eddies swept in on us. We saw ahead "willy-waws"—high white columns of spray—shoot across our bows to go hissing and whirling out to sea. These violent squalls were leaping down from the ice upland, through a break in the cliffs ahead of us. As we came abreast of this we had to keep so close in that the *Wills* was swept in by a swell and narrowly escaped being stove in against the rocks.

The looms of the oars became coated with frozen

spray, so that the rowers had difficulty in holding them with frostbitten hands. The slippery grip made it awkward to throw full weight into the rowing. Even so, Macklin broke an oar by hard pulling, and the *Stancomb Wills* suffered a similar mishap. That reduced our total stock of oars to twelve. The *James Caird,* being the heaviest and highest boat, was compelled to keep five oars to prevent being blown out to sea. We had four left, but the *Wills* had only three.

We were leading when I noticed that the *Wills* was falling astern in the squalls. I dropped back and handed our shortest oar to Crean, who was over six feet tall. He thanked me emphatically. "Skipper darlin'," he added, "what the hell's the good o' givin' me, the longest man, the shortest oar." "Swap it," I shouted, which he did. I then fervently exhorted my crew to "Pull your damnedest in spells an' relieve each other smartly." They did so well that we held our own, but without the herculean efforts of Macklin, Greenstreet, and McLeod we would have been blown out to sea.

The labour was so heavy that it warmed the men's hands enough to melt the ice off the looms. Before this we had a mishap. One frostbitten man could not hold his oar. It slipped from his grasp, broke the lanyard, and fell into the sea. "Back all," I yelled, but Kerr, sitting beside me, cleverly caught it before it passed astern. By the time Cheetham had relieved the frostbitten one and the three oars were in full swing again we were fifty yards astern of the other boats.

After two hours of hard pulling we struggled into the head of a gully that was scarcely more than a crack in the rocks but afforded us some shelter. Two men taking turns at the oars in each boat managed to hold us in position while we ate our cold rations and enjoyed a smoke.

After every man had rested and fed Shackleton gave the order to proceed. Although the gale was abeam we dared not set sail, for the squalls, blowing off the cliffs, eddied fiercely in all directions, and would almost certainly have capsized our small, undecked sailing boats. Clear of the gully the wind shrieked down on us, lashing the sea to white foam and tossing sheets and columns of spray high aloft.

Hanging on to the shelter of the cliffs as long as we could, we pulled inshore at an angle to the wind so that we drifted crabwise towards our destination.

Having only three oars, the *Docker*'s progress became still more crablike. While the other two boats managed to weather a rocky pillar 1,000 feet high that stood 200 yards offshore, we fell to leeward of it. There was a strong probability of the boat being driven out to sea. I vehemently urged the men to pull and pull harder. I became so fiercely insistent that, with the increase of wind, one man's nerve went. He growled and almost whined. Though patient enough normally, I lost my temper that time and raised the tiller ready. The suggestion was enough. He threw his weight on to the oar and saved his breath by ceasing to growl.

We were slowly drifting offshore and becoming desperate. I threw Marston into the fray to double bank the single oar on the weather side. I swore encouragingly at them and swung to them like a Cambridge cox.

We held our own, but made no headway. I urged them "Lay back! Lay back! Pull harder than you can pull." Illogical—like the Finn's "seesu"—but they did it. The boat gained a foot or two, but it was not enough. Having been steering I was the freshest, so I spelled Greenstreet at the stroke oar. "Take her and steer for the rock," I shouted, and went mad. I swore we would "Get to wind'ard or sink the bitch." "Fresh beef to the other oars," yelled Greenstreet. Macklin and Kerr seized the oars without losing a stroke, and the three of us went berserk. "Lay back! Lay back! you ——!" roared Greenstreet. We did "lay back," as not one of us had ever done before or ever did again. "Give it to her, we're gaining," shouted Greenstreet. "Lay back! Ram that rock! Up together! Lift her! Lift her." We "lifted" her. The boat drew ahead—drew ahead—drew a little more ahead. Half an hour later we were learning over our oars, gasping for breath and sweating in the lee of the great rock. We fell away from the oars to let Cheetham and Marston hold the boat in position. Greenstreet, with great judgment, kept her close in out of the wind, but did not let her touch the sheer face of the rock. The swell tossed us within an oar's length of the great cliff up which we seemed to climb dizzily for fifteen feet before sliding away from the rock as we fell in the trough of the sea.

Gradually our utter exhaustion was exchanged for relief. We were safe for a time. We grinned feebly at each other. The gale howled round the rock and went whistling past out to sea. Forty yards away on both sides the sea was streaked white with foam and spindrift.

As we rested and recovered our strength we watched and hoped for a lull—however brief—to give the boat a slant to cross to the shore. With the three oars out we waited.

At last there was a distinct decrease in the gale. Driving the boat ahead as hard as we could, we pulled out into the turmoil. Half an hour of hard pulling placed us close in where the coast trended more to the north. This allowed us to bring the wind behind the port beam, and we drove along with much less exertion.

Before 6 P.M. we sighted the landing ahead, where we saw the other boats being hauled ashore.

We reached the beach in the flaming glow of an amazingly beautiful but stormy sunset. Two great black crags to the west towered above the camp, their bases hidden in a crimson mist. To the southwest the roseate cliffs of a great glacier shone high above the storm-tossed waters of the bay. Our men ashore carrying stores up the beach looked like toiling ants. Suddenly they looked round, saw us and came down to help. Shackleton had been very anxious about our safety, and expressed his pleasure that we had arrived.

Under his directions the boats were unloaded and hauled up alongside the stores above high-water mark. Before the tents were pitched our dear black-faced Doughballs had made us a welcome pot of hot milk. He then cooked a hoosh, which put fresh life in all of us. After this we made camp and turned in.

Meantime the gale was blowing as hard as ever. Our threadbare tent had not been improved by the two boat passages. In the very early hours it ripped, as

Greenstreet expressed it, "From deadeye to breakfast time." Three of the inhabitants took their sleeping bags to the refuge of the other tents. Leaning out of my bag, I lifted the tent pole and shouted, "Look out, boys. Wrap the tent over your bags." Down came the pole. We pulled the tattered remains around us and at once fell fast asleep. We were quite comfortable under the snow, which before daylight had drifted a foot deep above us.

Gales of wind off the ice sheet blew almost incessantly. In one heavy gale sheets of ice a quarter-inch thick and a foot square were hurled about by the wind, making it dangerous to venture out.

After the tents were ruined we lived under the up-turned boats. The aristocracy slept in their bags on oars and sledge runners placed on the thwarts. On the dirt and blubber-caked shingle three feet beneath, the rougher Bolshevik element insolently reclined. The swells above knocked out their pipes or dropped dirty socks on the lower classes. This sometimes caused a slight unpleasantness which, fortunately, never culminated in a class war.

In that narrow gloomy space McIlroy and Macklin performed an amazing operation. They amputated Blackborrow's frostbitten toes, saving his foot and possibly his life. This record operation was a success in spite of the awful conditions the surgeons had to contend with.

This humble dwelling comprised bedroom, smoke room, dining room, operating theatre, and hospital. Shackleton once remarked, "If you wanted to go from one room to the other, you stopped where you were."

Seriously, I was always sorry for the twenty-two men who lived in that horrible place for four months of misery while we were away on the boat journey, and the four attempts at rescue ending with their joyful relief.

PART II

Shackleton's Boat Journey

I

We were twenty-eight men facing winter on a bleak, barren beach of Elephant Island. There was, at intervals, a possibility of fatal shortage of food, when seals or penguins failed to land from pack ice or the sea, or abandoned the rookery where such a dangerous neighbour as man had suddenly settled. But food insufficient for twenty-eight men might still nourish twenty-two, if six went for help.

There was nothing to suggest to the outside world that Sir Ernest Shackleton and his men were near the South Shetland group; rather would they look for us in the southern part of the Weddell Sea. There was no hope of rescue by others.

Plainly, the thing to do was to take a boat to the nearest inhabited point, risking the lives of a few for the preservation of the party.

It was certain that a man of such heroic mind and self-sacrificing nature as Shackleton would undertake this most dangerous and difficult task himself. He was, in fact, unable by nature to do otherwise. Being a born leader, he had to lead in the position of most danger, difficulty and responsibility. I have seen him turn pale, yet force himself into the post of greatest peril. That was his type of courage; he would do the job that he was most afraid of.

Before the *Endurance* was crushed and sunk, I had, as captain, worked out the courses and distances from the South Orkneys to South Georgia, the Falklands and Cape Horn respectively, and from Elephant Island to the same places.

From 55° to 60° S is the usual battleground of two great wind systems—the brave circumpolar westerlies and the polar easterlies; but around Elephant Island the westerlies are forced farther south by the thrust and deflection of the Andes and Cape Horn.

The westerly gales in the area that we proposed to cross are almost unceasing in the winter and cause strong east-running currents. This meant that we had practically no hope of reaching Cape Horn—the nearest point—and very little of making the Falklands, but would have fair gales and favouring currents to South Georgia.

It would have been impossible to have kept the twenty-eight men alive for that distance. The three boats could not have kept together, and the smaller two would probably have foundered. We therefore concentrated our meagre resources on the largest boat, the *James Caird,* so named by Shackleton after the principal supporter of his expedition. She was double-ended and clinker-built to my orders in July 1914, by

Messrs. W. J. Leslie, of Coldharbour, Poplar. Her planking was Baltic pine, keel and timbers American elm, stem and sternpost English oak. She was more lightly built than is required by the Board of Trade. This made her springy and buoyant. To make room for men and stores we removed the Muntz metal tanks fitted in her as a lifeboat.

While drifting on the pack ice, after the loss of the *Endurance,* the carpenter had built her 15 inches higher, constructed a whaleback at each end and fitted a pump made from the Flinders bar casing of the ship's compass. We launched the boat into a pool and loaded her with 2 1/3 tons' weight—about the same as on the great journey, which left her with 2 feet 2 inches freeboard, *i.e.,* height above water.

Marston, the artist, assisted with the alterations. Being stuck for something to "pay" her seams with, after they had been caulked with cotton lampwick, he used his oil colours, finishing off with seal's blood. This worked fairly well. It was probably the first time that artist's colours had been used for paying a boat's seams. Five months later, in the six days' journey through the ice to Elephant Island, she, with the other two boats, was well tested under most strenuous and stormy conditions. At that time she got holed by striking ice, and was repaired with a small patch of metal.

The carpenter, a splendid shipwright, could have made, if timber had been available, a cutter in which we could safely have carried the whole party. At Elephant Island he covered the space between the whalebacks with very limited materials, consisting of sledge runners, lids of boxes, and old canvas. Frozen like a board and caked with ice, the canvas was sewn, in painful circumstances, by two cheery optimists— Greenstreet, Chief Officer of the *Endurance,* and Bakewell, a Canadian AB. The only way they could do it was by holding the frozen canvas in the blubber fire till it thawed, often burning their fingers, while the oily smoke got in their eyes and noses, half-blinding and choking them. Then they sewed, often getting frostbitten and having to use great care that the difficult sewing with cold, brittle sail needles did not break all of our now scanty supply. All the time, while repeating the unpleasant task of thawing a length, and sewing it, "Horace" was irrepressibly cracking his sailor jokes and Bakewell replying.

Strange, nautical oaths, quips, and jests that would have made "The Pink 'Un" blush, flew to and fro. When finished it was a good job, and saved our lives more than once. A space was left at the after-end to steer from and give access to the "cabin."

The carpenter bolted one of the other boat's masts inside the keel of the *Caird* to prevent her breaking her back in extra heavy seas. The *Stancomb Wills*'s mast and sail were cut down to make a mizenmast and sail for the *Caird.* Her sails then were: jib, standing lug, and a small mizen. Had there been enough canvas I would have preferred the jib and lug only, the latter with a long foot. Ship's boats grip to windward and the mizen, when set, kept her so much in the wind that the rudder was always dragged across to keep her off. It was in the way, forced us to use a yoke instead of a tiller, and being a third sail was a third source of misery, especially when it and its gear got iced up. The

98

shrouds of the mainmast were secured with four brass screws two inches long.

The boat's gear consisted of four oars, six crutches, a long rope for painter and for dragging the sea anchor, a Navy boat's compass, an oil bag, red lights, flaming matches, two water breakers, a baler, two axes, a marlinespike, and a repair bag. We also took a "Primus," with paraffin and methylated spirits, seal oil, and a "medicine chest"—a small sledging outfit of Burroughs & Wellcome.

Sir Ernest had all possible improvements carried out in the boat and all preparations made for the journey.

Having, after consultation with Wild and myself, decided on making the journey, he selected to accompany him: Tom Crean, H. McNeish, Timothy Macarty, J. Vincent, and myself. Crean was a naval petty officer and Vincent a North Sea fisherman. The rest were Royal Naval Reserve and merchant service men.

Every day I watched closely for the sun or stars to appear, to correct my chronometer, on the accuracy of which our lives and the success of the journey would depend.

Never a gleam of sun or stars showed through the dull grey or else storm-driven pall of clouds that in these latitudes seems ceaselessly and miserably to shroud the bright blue sky and the cheerful light of sun or moon.

It was late in April; the southern winter was upon us. Daily, while watching for the sun, I went up the 150-foot rock to the north of the camp to watch the extent and movement of the ice starting to drift past the

99

island on the northeast current. Broken-up floes and streams of ice—scouts and skirmishers of the vanguard of the Great White Fleet—had already appeared. Borne each year from their icy fastnesses in the Antarctic by the broad stream that pours up through Bransfield Strait, they spread out in the winter through spillways of the South Shetlands, enveloping Clarence and Elephant Islands for weeks at a time.

On April 22 a broad band of ice lay along the north coast about two miles offshore. By St. George's Day it had extended to the east and threatened to surround the island.

Sir Ernest came up with me that day, and we discussed how to get through it. At our feet lay a narrow channel, separating us from a rocky islet 200 feet high. At our backs, behind the camp, were black, forbidding cliffs and blue, menacing glacier fronts. Grounded bergs indicated shoal patches, but troubled us not at all. They served us well by breaking the line of stream ice and making two gaps, one of which looked a promising opening through the imprisoning ice chain that encircled this isle of desolation. To the northwest, at intervals, a spouting white outburst showed where the treacherous nor'west breaker lay—twenty-two miles distant, two acres in extent, and ten miles offshore.

All was ready to launch and load the *Caird.* About fifteen hundredweight of shingle ballast had been sewn up in roughly-made canvas bags by Greenstreet, cheerfully profane as ever, Bakewell and How. This, with another five hundredweight of large stones, was piled just above high-water mark.

Sir Ernest decided that, if possible, we would start next day, and gave Wild instructions that, in the event of our not returning to relieve them before November, the opening of the whaling season at Deception Island, 140 miles distant, he was to assume that we were lost and make for that station.

Two of the men stayed up all night melting glacier ice over a blubber fire, and filling the two barricoes, or breakers, as seamen call them, with water. They also quarried, and left handy, several large blocks of ice for first use on the passage.

On Easter Monday, April 24, 1916, at 6 A.M., all hands turned out to "lash up and stow." While breakfast was cooking the *James Caird* was hauled close down to the sea ready for launching. The smaller boats were got ready to carry off ballast and stores to the *Caird* as soon as she was afloat.

Thirty days' food, water, and oil, and methylated spirits for the "Primus" were placed handy, as well as a tin of almost black seal oil, our six sleeping bags, and a bag of spare clothing. Sea boots and oilskins were nonexistent. They had long before been worn out, cut up, or used for other purposes.

Immediately after breakfast the sun came out obligingly. The first sunny day with a clear enough horizon to get a sight for rating my chronometer.*

I jubilantly welcomed this opportune appearance of

---

* This English chronometer, an excellent one of Smith's, was the sole survivor, in good going order, of the twenty-four with which we set out in the *Endurance*. [*Author's Note*]

the sun, for without it we should have been placed in a still more dangerous and difficult position making South Georgia.

After taking the sight, I went to the top of the lookout hill for a final study of the ice. It had moved to five or six miles offshore and was drifting northeast with wind and current. The gap had not closed up. Everything seemed promising for our start. The weather was clear, the sun shone at intervals, and the wind was moderate from the west. The long, unending westerly swell had eased down to a lazy heaving that, running round our rocky lookout point, made only a moderate surge in the eastern bay, instead of the heavy surf that had roared for the last week.

By nine o'clock the surf had increased slightly. After waiting an hour, there being no improvement, all hands launched the *Caird.* As she entered the sea a large roller caught, and almost capsized her, throwing McNeish and Vincent into the sea. I held out an oar to them in turn, and pushed them ashore into safety. Macarty and I then turned our attention to anchoring her. This done, I crawled down under the cover to find out why she was half-full of water. The plug had been knocked up, probably during the bumping on the rocks, and the sea was pouring in through the plug-hole. In the semidarkness I could not find the plug, so took a treasured possession of mine—pathetic remnant of civilization—a "white" handkerchief, now of a repelling dark griminess, wrapped it around a marlinespike and jammed it in the plughole. I held it there till Macarty was free to come down and assist to bale her out. After this we soon found the plug, jammed it in very firmly, and then felt that all was well again.

Having baled the water out, we stowed the ton of ballast along the bottom of the boat, as it was ferried off by the other two boats. It was too much by about five hundredweight. The overweighting was the cause of the *Caird's* slowness, stiffness, and jerky motion. It kept us constantly wet all the passage, so causing much unnecessary misery. I demurred strongly to Sir Ernest, but other counsels prevailed. He, knowing the danger of underballasting, went to the other extreme.

The unpleasant job of stowing the ballast in her gloomy little cavern was finished. The stores were ferried off and stowed. Our sleeping bags, spare clothes, oars, my sextant and navigation books were next handed in, then the two breakers of water and the lumps of ice. Unfortunately one of the breakers got stove in while hauling it off through the increasing surf, and a quantity of sea water, mixing with the fresh, partly spoiled it, as, to our cost, we found out later on.

As each boatload came alongside, the contents were passed to us, with a running fire of jokes, chaff, and good wishes from dear pals whom we were leaving behind. Many were solicitous that I might not overeat myself, and that my behaviour on reaching civilization should be above reproach. As for Crean, they said things that ought to have made him blush; but what would make Crean blush would make a butcher's dog drop its bone.

Sir Ernest, after some final instructions to Wild, came on board.

A few handshakes, we set sail, let go the mooring line, and started.

Cheers, yells, and arm-wavings from the boats and shore were answered by us to the full extent of our lungs.

It was half an hour past noon. I steered north for the open sea. We were off. The sun shone, the sea sparkled, a fresh west wind blew, and our spirits were high.

Elephant Island was opening out astern in majesty of glittering snowy peaks and uplands, fronted by glacier walls and towering cliffs. To the east, Cornwallis and Clarence Islands were revealed—two beautiful, serene, and stately virgins—with soft mauve wreaths and veils of misty clouds around their brows and shoulders. Around us, droves and lines of gentoo penguins, with a few seals, reassured us that the party left behind would get food. We felt more comfortable in our minds.

Our speed was nearly three knots. We heeled a little to windward, and so as soon as we cleared the land, we shipped seas that wetted us—oilskins and sea boots being things of the past. This was our baptism—the beginning of the ordeal by water.

Two hours later we reached the stream of ice that we had seen from the lookout hill. We passed several bergs, some grounded. We turned east, ran before the wind along the stream of broken old pack, and looked for the gap before mentioned.

Great fragments and hummocks of very old floes, worn, broken-down, and melted into all sorts of grotesque and wondrous shapes, were heaving, bowing, curtseying, and jostling on the long westerly swell.

They rose and fell on the heaving sea, drawing deceptively apart, then closing with a thud that would have smashed our boat like a gas mantle between thumb and finger. Castles, towers, and churches swayed unsteadily around us. Small pieces gathered and rattled against the boat. Swans of weird shape pecked at our planks, a gondola steered by a giraffe ran foul of us, which much amused a duck sitting on a crocodile's head. Just then a bear, leaning over the top of a mosque, nearly clawed our sail. An elephant, about to spring from a Swiss châlet on to a battleship's deck, took no notice at all; but a hyena, pulling a lion's teeth, laughed so much that he fell into the sea, whereupon a sea boot and three real penguins sailed lazily through a lovely archway to see what was to do, by the shores of a floe littered with the ruins of a beautiful white city and surrounded by huge mushrooms with thick stalks. All the strange, fantastic shapes rose and fell in stately cadence, with a rustling, whispering sound and hollow echoes to the thudding seas, clear green at the water line, shading to a deep, dark blue far below, all snowy purity and cool blue shadows above.

There is a great fascination in watching hill after hill of snow-clad floes with weird but lovely shapes bearing down on you, then vanishing in the hollows, to reappear in endless succession.

An hour's run brought us to the gap, now strewn with lumps and fragments of ice. Turning north we sailed a little way through, but the clouts from the ice becoming too heavy we lowered the sails and pulled —uncomfortable work in a cramped position on top of our jury-rigged deck covering.

To our great relief we cleared the stream just before

dark, and set sail—Elephant Island a pale shadow astern. We passed a few more lumps till 10 P.M., after which we saw not a single piece of ice until we reached South Georgia. This was a pleasant surprise. We were well content to be finished with our stubborn white foe. We did not know that later we were to long for a lump to assuage our thirst.

As we cleared the stream, the wind shifted to the southeast, our starboard quarter. Sir Ernest wisely wanted me to make due north to avoid the ice and get less frigid weather.

He sent the others below to get some warmth and sleep in the reindeer-skin bags while we kept a sharp lookout for ice. I steered; he sat beside me. We snuggled close together for warmth, for by midnight the sea was rising, and every other wave that hit her came over, wetting us through and through. Cold and clear, with the Southern Cross high overhead, we held her north by the stars, that swept in glittering procession over the Atlantic towards the Pacific. While I steered, his arm thrown over my shoulder, we discussed plans and yarned in low tones. We smoked all night—he rolled cigarettes for us both, a job at which I was unhandy. I often recall with proud affection memories of those hours with a great soul.

We had been working hard all day since 6 A.M., but Shackleton was always wonderful at keeping awake for two or three days or even more if necessary. "We must get north, Skipper," he said. And then, "Do you think this sou'easter will hold for us to reach Cape Horn?" "No," I answered, "but we may reach the Falklands, though it is almost certain that the westerly gales and easterly currents will force us to South Georgia." Then, "Do you know I know nothing about boat sailing?" he said, and laughed. "All right, Boss," I replied, "I do, this is my third boat journey." This slightly ruffled him. "I'm telling you that I don't," he answered.

This was where his courage shone most. For me, used to boat work, surf landings, and every kind of craft, this passage was an adventure—a too uncomfortable and dangerous one—but still an adventure. To him, who had drifted gradually from the sea and become mainly a land explorer, it must have been more menacing, perhaps even appalling. He could well have stayed on Elephant Island, but, as he said, "Never for me the lowered banner, never the last endeavour." Always for him the forward post of danger.

Still no ice. As the sky paled in the east, my sleepy head betrayed me. I nodded, and yawned twice. Sir Ernest, faintly annoyed, said, "You're sleepy. Turn in." He steered while I slept for two hours.

At daylight Crean lit the "Primus" and we had breakfast. We thankfully spooned our hot "hoosh" down with an occasional shudder as another sea broke "on deck," ran through the canvas and down our necks. After the "hoosh" we had a biscuit, four lumps of sugar, then a cigarette, made from plug tobacco, rolled in tissue paper.

The worst feature of meals was insufficient headroom to sit upright. One has no idea, before making the experiment, how uncomfortable, even distressing, this is. The chest is pressed down on the stomach; one swallows with difficulty, and the food appears to have no room to go down. To ease matters, one leant first on one elbow and then on the other, and tried lying on stones and boxes, imagining one was a Roman emperor reclining luxuriously at an epicurean banquet.

We went "watch and watch," three men keeping four hours at a time, while the other three slept. Sir Ernest took one watch with Crean and McNeish, I the other with Macarty and Vincent.

There was no means of exercise, unless one counts crawling like an infant. We crept at the end of our watch straight into our sleeping bags, or rather those just vacated by the other watch, for if we tried to get into our own they were sometimes frozen, so we laid them beneath us on the boxes, in an attempt to soften the corners of the latter. The routine was: three men in bags deluding themselves that they were sleeping, and three men "on deck"; one man steering for an hour, while the other two, when not pumping, baling, or handling sails, were sitting in our "saloon" (the biggest part of the boat, where we all had grub). They smoked, discussed the weather, and talked of what they could eat and drink, not in any boastful spirit, but soberly and after mature deliberation. All the time streams of water ran through the canvas, down necks and backs. Those on watch sat as still as possible, because three minutes after a sea had wetted them the heat of their bodies warmed the chill out of the clothes on which they were sitting, but if they moved a quarter of an inch one way or the other they felt cold, wet garments on their flanks and sides. Sitting very still for a while, life was worth living—one could almost purr!

Then slosh! came another sea—"fisherman's luck—wet stern and no fish."

We knew it was cold, but did not carry a thermometer—it would only have made us colder. My height-recording aneroid, which was also a weatherglass, we kept in its case and never looked at—it would only have made us anxious, and we had but three sails to furl.

The twenty-fifth—the second day out. At daybreak we had made forty-five miles from Elephant Island, but the wind coming north, we stood west, so by noon we had made no more, or may have been driven back a little. The wind then hauled to west-southwest, and blew a gale with a great northwest swell and high "cross sea." This is a sailor's term for two seas from different directions running through or across one another, the result of two gales. It found out our weak spots nicely. The *Caird* was tumbling about with a hard, jerky motion and two or three bucketsful of each sea came icy-cold over us. Numerous penguins were swimming and leaping out of the water near the boat. They had been calling out during the night like lost souls.

I think all, except Macarty and myself, had been seasick. I certainly had felt squeamish. Now even the worst cases recovered. A bucket of icy water down the neck checks the fiercest vomiter. We gained further benefit from the task of pumping and baling the boat. It made us forget what worms we were.

We had stowed all stores to the best possible advantage on the ballast. Our sleeping bags were laid in the bows on top of food boxes, whose sharp corners stuck into our bodies in inconvenient and painful fashion. It was a strange cabin, seven feet long, five feet wide at one end, tapering to a point at the other. Barely room to sit up after crawling in through the narrow space between the ballast and stores below and the thwart above. What a crawl! It became a nightmare. The first part on hands and knees over sharp stones—nasty, knobbly stones and round stones over which you slipped off and on, the Southern Ocean meantime draining out of your clothes and finneskoe boots. Then came the passage! You braced yourself up—or rather down; crawling and wriggling on chest and stomach, you insinuated yourself between the ballast and the thwart. Halfway through you paused for breath—you became exhausted and doubted if life was worth living, but then came a gentle nudge from the next man's head or shoulder against your after-end, and you again moved reluctantly forward. This crawl in one side of the mast, out the other, of Weary Willies going below and Tired Tims coming "on deck" was such an operation that Sir Ernest took charge of the queue and directed the order of march.

Fortunately, the bow space, when gained, was penetrated only by the heaviest seas, so that the sleeping bags did not get thoroughly wet for two days, and then we could still generate a certain amount of warmth before the next extra heavy sea. Here we were lifted up and hurled down. With her bows and our bodies we whipped, swept, flailed, and stamped on the seas. Van Tromp and Blake weren't in it with us. We leaped on the swells, danced on them, flew over them, and dived into them. We wagged like a dog's tail, shook like a flag in a gale, and switchbacked over hills and dales. We were sore all over.

In a short time our ideas of size altered amusingly. We looked on our twenty-two-foot boat as quite sizable—talked of going for'ard or aft, of the watch coming on deck or going below, as though we were in a hundred-ton sailing craft. "Who's next wheel?" was frequently asked, forgetting for the moment that our craft was so small that we used yoke lines to work our rudder.

Sir Ernest ran the routine, "whacked out" stores and arranged mealtimes. We had hot milk every four hours at night—he couldn't quite manage a hot bath or a dry bed! I navigated and set the course to be steered—when we could steer it—a matter of guesswork at night. Crean cooked, that is, he boiled the water and stirred in the ration, while we fished out gatherings of reindeer hairs that had got in from the sleeping bags.

We all steered, reefed, furled or set sail, and pumped in turns.

One man had to hold down the pump's brass tube in icy-cold water at the bottom of the boat, while the other man worked the plunger up and down. The man holding the tube down had to use force to prevent the other man pulling it out of his hands. Our hands were unable, even slightly, to warm the tube, as there was a constant stream of cold water up inside. The seas that swept over us had to be pumped out every four hours—often every two—and between whiles we heard the water running about under the ballast in a most alarming manner.

By dark the weather was a little better. The great grey shroud that, for weeks on end, holds back God's sunshine from these sub-Antarctic waters was torn aside, the stars came out at intervals, and we checked the course once or twice an hour by an old friend called Antares—the Scorpion's red eye. When his beacon light was hidden by clouds, we steered by observing how the wind blew out our little blue pennant at the masthead. We had no spare candles for the compass—only one six inches long that I was saving for emergencies—principally making the coast. The moon was in her last quarter the night we sailed. In the morning we got a glimpse of her—the only one on the journey.

The third day it blew a hard west-southwest gale with snow squalls. Great torn cumulus and nimbus raced overhead. Heavy westerly seas rushing up on our port quarter swept constantly over the boat, pouring into the "cockpit" and coming through the canvas in little torrents, soaking everything. After this, for the rest of the passage, the only dry articles in the boat were matches and sugar in hermetically sealed tins.

I took observations of the sun for position, but the boat pitched, rolled, and jerked so heavily that I could take them only by kneeling on the after-thwart, with Macarty and Vincent clinging to me on either side, to prevent me pitching overboard, sextant and all. This sextant, one of Heath's, had been presented to Hudson, navigating officer of the *Endurance.* I found it more convenient for use in the boat than my own.

A few penguins were seen and heard through the day.

Stormy, snowy weather. Rolling, pitching, and tumbling, we laboured before the roaring grey-green seas that towered over us, topped with hissing white combers that alas! always caught us. Bruised and soaked, with never a long enough interval for our bodies to warm our streaming clothes, in zero weather we now fully gauged the misery and discomfort of our adventure.

It was "grin and bear it." Yet there was a great compensation: we were making good headway on our course.

We made, slightly aided by the current, 83 miles—128 from Elephant Island. As might be expected, my reckoning was wide of the mark. In the dark our course was most erratic, and at all hours the iron rod of the pump was working up and down within a few inches of the compass. However, after some practice at this style of navigation, I got some surprisingly close results.

The position at noon was 59° 46' south latitude, 52° 18' west longitude. I said to Sir Ernest "Thank goodness, we've finished with the sixties," but during the next two days we were nearly blown back over the sixtieth parallel.

After noon the wind backed to north, blew another gale, and so continued all that fourth day. The weather was overcast and misty, with hard squalls of wind and rain. It was a head wind; it was dangerous to stand too far east for fear of meeting ice. With all our efforts to beat to wind'ard, I reckoned that we were in the same position as the day before. This was disheartening. We were as much drenched as ever by seas sweeping over

113

us; and without the feeling that we were conquering distance. The current appeared to have been running east-southeast, from the absence of ice in an area where we expected it and the appearance of two pieces of wreckage, probably floated down from near Cape Horn.

II

I had previously managed to keep the books from getting wet, but that day my navigating books and log were in a pitiable state—soaked through, stuck together, illegible, and almost impossible to write in. They were not paper pulp, but something like it, and it took me all my time to open them without completely destroying all chance of navigating to land. Navigation is an art, but words fail to give my efforts a correct name. Dead reckoning or DR—the seaman's calculation of courses and distance—had become a merry jest of guesswork. Once, perhaps twice, a week the sun smiled a sudden wintry flicker, through storm-torn clouds. If ready for it, and smart, I caught it. The procedure was: I peered out from our burrow—precious sextant cuddled under my chest to prevent seas falling on it. Sir Ernest stood by under the canvas with chronometer, pencil, and book. I shouted, "Stand by," and knelt on the thwart—two men holding me up on either side. I brought the sun down to where the horizon ought to be and as the boat leaped frantically upward on the crest of a wave, snapped a good guess at the altitude and yelled, "Stop." Sir Ernest took the time, and I worked out the result. Then the fun started! Our fingers were so cold that he had to interpret his wobbly figures—my own so illegible that I had to recognize them by feats of memory. Three months later I could read only half of them. My navigation books had to be half-opened, page by page, till the right one was reached, then opened carefully to prevent utter destruction. The epitome had had the cover, front and back pages washed away, while the Nautical Almanac shed its pages so rapidly before the onslaught of the seas that it was a race whether or not the month of May would last to South Georgia. It just did, but April had vanished completely.

Part of our canvas covering was carried away by a sea. This slightly curtailed our "saloon," but, on the other hand, enlarged our "cockpit," so it was easier to pop our heads out and see the view.

The fifth morning we had a light northwest breeze, changing later to a strong westerly with overcast misty weather. High northwest and westerly swells kept the *Caird* busy with her usual violent jerking—"Roll, bowl, or pitch"—generally all three together. Sweeping seas came over us all day and maintained our moisture.

In the afternoon the swell settled and lengthened out—the typical deep-sea swell of these latitudes. Offspring of the westerly gales, the great unceasing westerly swell of the Southern Ocean rolls almost unchecked around this end of the world in the Roaring

Forties and the Stormy Fifties. The highest, broadest, and longest swells in the world, they race on their encircling course until they reach their birthplace again, and so, reinforcing themselves, sweep forward in fierce and haughty majesty, Four hundred, a thousand yards, a mile apart in fine weather, silent and stately they pass along. Rising forty or fifty feet and more from crest to hollow, they rage in apparent disorder during heavy gales. Fast clippers, lofty ships, and small craft are tossed on their foaming, snowy brows, and stamped and battered by their ponderous feet, while the biggest liners are playthings for these real Leviathans of the Deep, with a front of a thousand miles. Smitten, pounded and smothered by them, many a good ship has foundered with all hands; a tossing lifebuoy or a grating alone remaining to mark their grave.

At times, rolling over their allotted ocean bed, in places four miles deep, they meet a shallow of thirty to a hundred fathoms—the Birdwood Bank, near Cape Horn, the Agulhas off the Stormy Cape, and others. Their bases retarded by the bank, their crests sweep up in furious anger at this check, until their front forms an almost perpendicular wall of green, rushing water, that smashes on a ship's deck, flattening steel bulwarks, snapping two-inch steel stanchions, and crushing deckhouses and boats like eggshells. These blue-water hills in a very heavy gale move as fast as twenty-five statute miles an hour, but striking the banks, the madly leaping crests falling over and onward, probably attain a momentary speed of fifty miles or more. The impact of hundreds of tons of *solid* water at this speed can only fairly be imagined. Even on deeper banks they may be seen "topping up," for the disturbance of these huge rollers extends down a thousand feet at times. Born of the fierce, gloomy nor'wester, harrowed, combed and scourged by the devilish wrathful squalls of their sire, the sou'wester, they keep, in the main, to their easterly course. Even when meeting the sudden blast of the sou'easter's fury they still hold mightily on their way, their great crests blown back in long white streamers—the manes of the galloping white horses. Their sou'east foe may lead the attack for two or three days, and apparently stay their career, but they are never quite subdued, for as the gale eases they can still be seen moving east, though slowly, and when their head wind has died away, there they are, still pressing onward, unbeaten. They had only been hidden and disguised by the surface tumult of the sou'easter.

So we held our way; in those valleys and on those ridges alternately. First, half becalmed—a hill of water ahead, another astern—the following hill lifts us, and the boat slides with increasing speed down the ever-steepening slope, till with a sudden upward swoop, the sea boiling white around and over us, we are on the summit with a commanding view of a panorama of dark grey and indigo blue rollers, topped and broken with white horses. The crest passing leaves the boat apparently stationary, gravity now holding her back till the next hollow reaches us, and so on *ad nauseam.*

There was little variety, during bad weather, in our conversation. We spoke in set phrases: "What's it like?"—an inquiry regarding the weather from the watch coming on or someone below to the helmsman. "There's a hell of a sea." "She steers like a Dutch galliot." "Eight bells." "The sun's coming out, Skipper." "Look out for a big 'un!" "Pump ship!!" "Balers!!!" "Reef the mainsail!" "Keep her northeast." "Curse these stones." "And this is how the poor live." "A life on the ocean wave. Bah!" "Hoosh!!"

The position by DR was $59°52'S$, $51°46'W$. We had made only eighteen miles east-southeast—a bad direction. We were six miles farther south than we were two days before. This was the result of the northerly gale and the current. A disappointing result.

Poor Vincent was in great pain and trouble with his legs and feet. It appeared he'd had rheumatism on Elephant Island. The constant wetting did not improve matters. Sir Ernest gave him something from the medicine chest—witch hazel, I think—to rub in. The cure, of course, would have been dry clothes, but they were beyond reach.

Quoting from my diary:

"Pumping and baling boat every watch and at shorter intervals when the sea gets up. Crean is 'Primus' expert and chef, but it takes three of us to steady the 'Primus' and cooker against the boat's violent motion. The greatest trouble is the choking of the 'Primus' by dirt and reindeer hair from the sleeping bags (now moulting from continual wet) and the confined space. It consequently requires much more attention and pricking than on a sledging journey."

The procedure was: Crean pricked and lit the "Primus" and put his back against one side of the boat while I put mine against the other. We extended our legs towards each other till we could jam the "Primus" between our feet. Any deficiency in the length of my legs was made up for by Crean's excess. In this way we held the "Primus" firm on its base. We and that "Primus" would have been more difficult to dislodge than Whitehall limpets or conscientious objectors during the war. My unworthy hands held the aluminium cooker that was to receive the sacred hoosh, and my duty as scullion was swiftly, but reverently, to raise it on high whenever the boat gave a madder leap than usual, and so save the precious contents from spilling in the bilges or on the "Primus" flame. At the bidding of Crean, the High Priest of Cookery, and tender of the Sacred Flame, Macarty broke in the lumps of ice. When melted, Crean himself broke up and stirred in the ration—half a pound a man. All eyes, save the helmsman's, were glued on the cooker; hoosh pots and spoons were ready. As soon as it boiled Crean shouted, "Hoosh," and blew out the "Primus." The pots shot forward, Crean rapidly, but carefully, filling them in turn. We swallowed it scaldingly hot, having gradually trained mouths, throats, and stomachs to a pained acquiescence. So we felt the glorious heat going right through our chilled, numbed bodies and limbs, putting new life into us. The first to finish his hoosh jumped outside and relieved the helmsman so that he might take his while it was still hot.

Sir Ernest saw that each man had as much as he wanted, and after this course generally served out a quarter of a pound of Streimer's nut food, a large biscuit, and four lumps of sugar. It was his principle to fight the cold, and constant soaking, by ample hot food.

About this date Sir Ernest was troubled with sciatica and, at times, in great pain. It was hard to have such a painful complaint added to the miseries of the passage, but he showed his usual fortitude, never complained, looked after the men's comfort as much as ever, and even grinned at my chestnut of Pat's query to Mick, who said he'd come home and found his wife in bed with sciatica. "Did ye kill the Oitalian divvle?" Fortunately the sciatica cleared up in about four days.

By this time we were exceedingly dirty, our faces nearly black—our hands quite so—from blubber and soot. I remember once, while holding the cooker and absorbed in watching Crean stirring, I saw him stop and stare into the hoosh. I almost trembled! The next moment a filthy black paw shot out, seized a handful of reindeer hair from the hoosh, squeezed it out, so as to waste nothing, and then threw it away. We didn't mind a little dirt, but we drew the line at reindeer hair.

The sixth day it blew a west-southwest gale. Cloudy and misty. High lumpy sea. The boat pitched, rolled and jerked heavily, shipping seas all over her as usual, but we made a glorious run of ninety-two miles on a N 36° E course.

A fine run and a fine course, putting us well to the north and, we hoped, farther from cold weather. We had covered 238 miles since leaving Elephant Island, but not in a straight line. I got the sun again, the position being 58° 38′ south latitude, and 50° 0′ west longitude.

I remember my "trick" at the helm that night in the

middle watch. She rolled and plunged along in the dark; Sir Ernest's watch asleep or silent in their wet bags; my watchmates, Macarty and Vincent, smoking and talking in low tones in the black cavern under the canvas deck, until one should relieve me at the end of the hour.

Half standing, half sitting on the coaming of the cockpit, I steered by watching the angle at which the pennant blew out; at times verifying the course by a glimpse of a star through a rift in the clouds. Dark hills of water reared sudden and startling ahead and astern, capped by pale gleams of breaking seas. A hiss of water at the bows as she ran heeling down a long sea. Dark shapes of sails, overhead and forward, bellied out to leeward. Steering by the lee yoke-line only, to prevent her flying up in the wind, I gave it an extra tug, whenever startled by the roar of a breaking sea behind me, in the effort to prevent the water sweeping over us. Drenched through again and again, there was yet a certain fascination in holding her to her course and doing one's best to fight the elements, and get her to her destination.

Sunday, the last day of April, it blew a heavy southwest by south gale, with overcast weather. The temperature, no less than the compass, told us the wind was more southerly.

A heavy sea was making up, before which the boat ran badly, steering wildly and shipping heavy seas until noon, when we had to heave to by paying out the sea anchor on the end of the painter. After this she took very little water over.

The run was seventy-eight miles by DR.

After noon the gale and sea increased, with intense cold. We rolled the sails up and stowed them below in the already confined space, to prevent them freezing, holding a mass of ice and capsizing the boat with top weight. The seas breaking on the boat froze and cased her heavily with ice, but we should have been worse off without the sea anchor.

To keep a boat afloat in very heavy weather, two things are almost necessities—oil to mollify the seas, and a sea anchor to ride to. Of oil we had ample for one day's gale—we had ten days' gales on this passage. A sea anchor consists of a canvas cone or bag, three to four feet long, the mouth nearly as wide and a small hole at the other end. Four small lines at the mouth are spliced into a "thimble," to which the rope is attached. When a gale is so heavy that a boat cannot run before it, she takes in sail and heaves to by throwing the sea-anchor over, with one end of the rope passed through the thimble, and the other end fast in the bows. Having no other rope, we used the painter. By dragging in the sea—the water escaping through the small hole—the sea anchor holds the boat head to wind and sea, the best position for riding out a gale.

We saw a few penguins in the afternoon, three hundred miles from any land. They were quite indifferent to the gale or the cold; we felt envious of them. By the bitter cold of the gale we reckoned it blew straight off pack ice not far away.

We drank our seal oil, black and odoriferous, as it was not worth keeping for one day of the gale and its calories were so valuable. A matter of latitude—what would have made us ill in the tropics was nectar here!

The ice increased on the boat till we had to excavate the four oars from a mound of it. They caught so much freezing water that we were forced to throw two overboard, and lash the others one on each side, for a railing from the mainshrouds to the mizenmast, eighteen inches above the "deck." They held very little ice then, and there was less danger of falling overboard. This was a serious sacrifice, but we could not get the other two oars below.

All night the breaking seas froze over her. This had one advantage; it stopped intermittent bucketsful pouring through the "deck" and down our necks, but pumping and baling had still to be done at frequent intervals.

The eighth day the gale held steadily throughout from south-southwest, with a very heavy, lumpy sea. It was impossible to write—even a few remarks. These would have been illegible—but anyway unprintable—owing to the violent jerky contortions of the *Caird.* She was heavily iced all over outside, and a quantity of ice had formed inside her.

Sir Ernest had the "Primus" going day and night as long as we could stand the fumes, then it would be put out for an hour. This and a generous drink of life-giving hot milk every four hours, at the relief of the watches, kept all hands from any ill effects.

All gear was wet through. The sleeping bags had a nasty sour-bread kind of smell, and were on the point of fermenting. I believe, in fact, that a certain amount of fermentation had started, and so prevented us feeling the cold quite so much in our sleep, as we called it.

We all smelt as well, or rather as ill, as our bags. We used to long for a hot bath or clean, dry clothes.

May Day. The ice on the boat got so thick and heavy that she was riding deep and had a tendency to capsize. Something had to be done, and quickly, so we took it in turns to crawl out with an axe and chop off the ice. What a job! The boat leaped and kicked like a mad mule; she was covered fifteen inches deep in a casing of ice like a turtleback, with slush all over where the last sea was freezing. First you chopped a handhold, then a kneehold, and then chopped off ice hastily but carefully, with an occasional sea washing over you. After four or five minutes—"fed up" or frostbitten—you slid back into shelter, and the next man took up the work. It was a case of "one hand for yourself, and one for the King," for if a man had gone overboard then, it would have been good-bye. Finally, we got the bulk of it off, and were satisfied. All night the gale continued heavily from south-southwest.

The ninth day. In the forenoon a heavy sea struck the *Caird*. Almost immediately her bows fell off till the sea was abeam. The great cake of ice that had formed on the painter at the bows, in such a position that we could not smash it off, had swung to and fro, round and round, till it had sawed and chafed through the painter. So we lost both rope and sea anchor, which seemed a double disaster to us.

We beat the ice off the jib, reefed and set it on the mainmast.

By 11 A.M. the gale had eased enough for us to set the reefed lug and jib and run drunkenly before the wind and sea.

This fierce, cold gale had lasted at its height for forty-eight hours. During that period we had, no fewer than three times—once practically in the dark—to crawl out on top of the boat to chop and scrape the ice off. We all agreed it was the worst job we had ever taken on in our lives.

I estimated that day's drift at thirty-six miles—sixty-six miles to northeast during the time we were hove to. The boat's antics were almost as bad as before. The dead reckoning figures were made one at a time by jabbing with the pencil as occasion offered. By strict economy I confined their numbers to twenty-five. It was impossible to write—perhaps I should say it was impossible to force oneself to try.

The reindeer bags were now so miserable to get into that when we had finished our watch and it was time to turn in, we had serious doubts as to whether it was worth while. The smell of cured skin constantly soaked and slept in was appalling. First you undressed; that is, you took off your boots, and throwing back the flap of the bag thrust your legs in hurriedly. It felt like getting between frozen rawhide—which it was. You kicked your feet violently together for two minutes to warm them and the bag, then slid in to the waist. Again you kicked your feet and knocked your knees together and then like a little hero made a sudden brave plunge right inside. At first, while you knocked your feet together, it felt like an icehouse, and then it began to thaw out and you wished it hadn't—it smelt so, and the moulting hairs got into eyes, mouth, and nose. So, coughing, sneezing, and spluttering, you kicked your feet valiantly together till there was enough warmth in them to allow you to sleep for perhaps an hour. When you awoke you kicked again till you fell asleep, and so on.

After this gale the bags were in such a hopeless, sloppy, slimy mess, and weighed so heavily, that Sir Ernest had the worst two thrown overboard.

All that day and night we held on our erratic course before the gale.

In steering a small boat before a heavy gale don't look back—it may disconcert you. Fix your eye on a cloud or breaking sea right ahead and keep her straight—if you can. When you hear a roaring Bull of Bashan, with a wet nose, galloping up behind you, keep your shoulders hunched up to your ears—till you get it, then yell, "Pump and balers." There's no need to, for they're hard at it already, but it shows you're alive, all right.

A great find—an inch of candle in the socket of the compass lamp. At night I lit it, and dropping a few spots of grease on the compass glass, stuck it three inches to the right of the centre. Then the procedure was to strike a flaming match once a watch at night for a smoke, and to light this piece of candle for a few minutes. Sheltered by our hands, its flickering light enabled the helmsman to correct the course and check it off by the sea, wind, and fluttering pennant. No need to blow it out, the wind did that, then all was darkness again, except for Tom Crean or Macarty's dully glowing pipe. About this time the compass glass got broken. We mended it with strips of sticking plaster from the medicine chest.

After my "trick" at the helm in the middle watch,

when extra cold and wet, I got stiffened in the crouching position I had assumed to dodge the seas, and had to be hauled inside, massaged, and opened out like a jackknife before I could get into my sleeping bag.

A few scribbled remarks in my navigating book ran: "Bags and finneskoe moulting at a great rate—'feathers' everywhere—most objectionable in hoosh. My finneskoe are now quite bald. We are all suffering from superficially frostbitten feet, Macarty is the most irrepressible optimist I've ever met. When I relieved him at the helm, boat iced over and seas pouring down our necks, one came right over us and I felt like swearing, but just kept it back, and he informed me with a cheerful grin 'It's a foine day, sorr.' I had been feeling a bit sour before, but this shamed me. His cheeriness does brighten things up."

As a rule, when a sea wets a sailor through, he swears at it, and comprehensively and impartially curses everything in sight, beginning with the ship and the "old man"—if he's not within hearing; but on this passage we said nothing when a sea hit us in the face. It was grin and bear it; for it was Sir Ernest's theory that by keeping our tempers and general cheeriness we each helped to keep one another up. We all lived up to this to the best of our ability, but Macarty was a marvel.

After the third day our feet and legs had swelled, and began to be superficially frostbitten from the constant soaking in sea water, with the temperature at times nearly down to zero; and the lack of exercise. During the last gale they assumed a dead-white colour and lost surface feeling.

Our footgear consisted of two pairs of Jaeger wool socks, homemade felt shoes, ankle-high (mine were Greenstreet's handiwork), and, over all, finneskoe (reindeer-skin boots), hair out and skin in, when we started—now it was skin inside and out. When your feet got unbearably cold you took off your footgear and, rinsing your socks in the sea, wiped your feet, wrung out your socks, and again wiped your feet before replacing your footgear. This was the wag's opportunity. While busily engaged with your socks he would prick your toe with a "Primus" pricker. Getting no response he would prick higher and higher up foot and leg, till the victim suddenly jumped, yelled, or swore according to temperament. This was not merely horseplay or idle curiosity—it was also an index as to how one's feet and legs were standing the rigours of the passage.

To prevent my feet getting worse, I adopted a system of wriggling them constantly, contracting and relaxing my toes until quite tired, waiting a minute, then wriggling them again, and so on. I think it saved my feet a good deal.

At midnight Shackleton relieved me. The southwest gale had been steadily increasing with snow squalls for eight hours and there was a heavy cross sea running which caused us to ship more seas over the boat even than usual. Just before he crawled out from under the canvas a sea struck me full in the face and the front as I stood aft steering with the lee yoke line to keep her out of the wind. The water was running out of me as he relieved me at the helm and then another sea dashed over the two of us. "Pretty juicy," he said, and we both forced a laugh. I crawled below and into my sodden sleeping bag. In spite of wet and cold I fell asleep instantly, but soon after something awakened me. Then I heard Shackleton shout "It's clearing, boys!" and immediately after, "For God's sake, hold on! It's got us!" The line of white along the southern horizon that he had taken for the sky clearing was, in fact, the foaming crest of an enormous sea. I was crawling out of my bag as the sea struck us. There was a roaring of water around and above us—it was almost as though we had foundered. The boat seemed full of water. We other five men seized any receptacle we could find and pushed, scooped, and baled the water out for dear life. While Shackleton held her up to the wind, we worked like madmen, but for five minutes it was uncertain whether we would succeed or not.

We could not keep that pace up—gradually we eased off as we realized that we had saved our lives. With the aid of the little homemade pump and two dippers it took us nearly an hour to get rid of the water and restore the boat to her normal state of having only a few gallons of water washing about the bilges through the stones and shingle. The wave that had struck us was so sudden and enormous that I have since come to the conclusion that it may have been caused by the capsizing of some great iceberg unseen and unheard by us in the darkness and the heavy gale.

The tenth day. In the morning the southwest gale moderated and backed to west with great white cumulus clouds racing overhead, and clear weather. "Old Jamaica" showed his face through the clouds and I made the position 56°13'S and 45°38'W. The run was

$N55°E$ sixty-two miles, 444 since leaving Elephant Island. We had done more than half the distance, and had a happy feeling of certainty that we should succeed in our adventure.

After noon the wind hauled to south-southeast and fell light. The weather became bright and clear, with a few passing clouds and splendid warming spells of sunshine that we revelled in. It was the first good day of the passage. The few seas shipped we managed to dodge. We turned the four sleeping bags inside out, hanging them and our clothing on masts, halyards, and rigging, and were able to alter their condition from wet to damp—a pleasant change. We were a ragged, tough-looking crew of cutthroat appearance. We didn't care—we were happy. By sunset it was blowing a strong southeast breeze with fine, clear, cold weather as we steered northeast with the wind abeam.

The pennant had gradually blown away until it was invisible in the dark, which made it still more difficult to hold the boat near her course.

III

Our eleventh day was splendid—a day's grace. Moderate southeast breezes. Blue sky and passing clouds. The sea was moderate, and the great long westerly swell went shouldering lazily across us. We only shipped an occasional small sea, and, again hanging out our gear, got it into a pleasantly moderate state of dampness. We felt very uppish indeed that night, when we crawled into our sleeping bags and thought with pity of our unfortunate pals on Elephant Island, though they were probably pitying us at that moment.

The day before I had taken observations of the sun, cuddling the mast with one arm and swinging fore and aft round the mast, sextant and all. This day I found the best way was, sitting on the deck, to jam one foot between the mast and halyards, the other against the shroud, and catch the sun when the boat leaped her highest on the crest of a sea, allowing the "height of

133

eye" accordingly. Position $55°31'S$, $44°43'W$, run N36°E fifty-two miles; total 496.

From my navigation book: "In assisting with the 'Primus' I burn my fingers on the aluminium rest for the cooker. My subsequent antics with the crumpled-up thing that now bears a faint resemblance to a lady's hat that I am endeavouring to trim, sends everyone into yells of laughter, in which, after a while, I cannot help joining too." This was quite the heartiest laugh we had on the passage, helped, no doubt, by the two good days we had enjoyed. We had one other good laugh, but I cannot now remember what it was about.

The twelfth day a southeast breeze blew strong on the starboard beam. It was clear weather, but overcast and squally, with a lumpy sea and southwest swell. We shipped seas. Everything was wet through again.

Our plug tobacco had gradually disintegrated and washed apart into its original leaves, which were carried by the water under and to and fro through the ballast. Sometimes, with the aid of reindeer hair, they choked the pump. Sea-sodden pieces were salvaged by the seamen, and, while Crean and I were operating the "Primus," laid on the crumpled rest previously mentioned to be dried or scorched.

After meals the leaves that had not found their way into the hoosh were torn up, shredded and laboriously rolled with toilet paper into a cigarette. Macarty or Vincent then performed prodigies of drawing at it, and when at a dull glow handed it, as a special treat, to Sir Ernest, who, not liking to hurt anyone's feelings, took it gingerly, puffed away for a minute and, when the donor's back was turned, slyly handed it to Crean, who puffed valiantly for a while. It was often too strong even for him, and so by degrees found its way back to the maker, who finished it with gusto.

From the ceaseless cold and soaking we suffered much bodily inconvenience. The constant chafing of wet clothes had also made our thighs sore and inflamed. One thing we were spared, that was small lodgers—too wet and cold for them.

That day was the *James Caird*'s biggest twenty-four hours' run, N50°E ninety-six miles; but being by dead reckoning it may have been a little less or a little more. Wallis Island, at the west end of South Georgia, bore N80°E 155 miles. It sounded quite close to us. Our position was 54°30′S, 42°36′W.

The thirteenth day was also clear but overcast, with a north by west gale and a heavy, lumpy sea that increased so much after noon that we were forced to heave to with the reefed jib on the mainmast. Since leaving Elephant Island I had only been able to get the sun four times, two of these being mere snaps or guesses through slight rifts in the clouds.

Our hands had become awful objects to look upon. Crean's and mine, in addition to being almost black with grime, blubber, and soot, were ornamented with recent frostbites, also burns from the "Primus." Each successive frostbite on a finger was marked by a ring where the skin had peeled up to, so that we could count our frostbites by the rings, after the method of a woodman telling the age of a tree.

From the day after leaving Elephant Island we had been accompanied at intervals by albatross, the stateliest bird in flight in the world, and mollyhawks, a smaller species of albatross. These birds, peculiar to the Southern Ocean, are only seen as far south as the edge of the pack ice. Their northern limit is $30°S$, though I once saw both a few miles within the tropics to the south of St. Helena, following the cool current. The albatross is sometimes divided into two species, the Wandering and the Royal, the latter slightly larger, though it is possibly only an older bird of the same species. Their usual spread of wings from tip to tip is about eleven feet. I have measured a Royal fourteen feet across, and there is one in the Adelaide Museum that is given as sixteen feet! This gives them the largest span of wing of any bird in the world.

Awkward on the land, ludicrous when struggling to rise from a smooth sea, the albatross is most graceful and stately on the wing. He sweeps before the gale with a mighty rush, then, turning sharply, lets the wind strike his underside, soars almost perpendicularly, and again turns with the wind, coming down in a long, symmetrical swoop, carelessly lifting a few inches to clear the top of a breaking sea, while conforming his flight to the surface of the ridges and hollows. He is a noble sight when the white cross of his back, shoulders, neck, and rump shows startlingly against the heavy black of an advancing squall.

Never seeming to rest, week after week, he follows the sailing ship; day after day he followed our boat. His poetic motion fascinated us; the ease with which he swept the miles aside filled us with envy. He could, with a southwest gale, have made our whole journey in ten hours.

In some of the few fine watches we had, Crean made

noises at the helm that, we surmised, represented "The Wearin' o' the Green." Another series of sounds, however, completely baffled us.

I sang—Macarty thought it was a recitation—that classic:

> *She licked him, she kicked him,*
> *She wouldn't let him be;*
> *She welted him, and belted him,*
> *Until he couldn't see.*

> *But Macarty wasn't hearty;*
> *Now she's got a different party.*
> *She might have licked Macarty,*
> *But she* can't lick me.

The last part triumphantly to Macarty, but I doubt if he believed it. Then I sang "We're Bound for the Rio Grande." No one complained. It's astonishing how long-suffering people become on a trip like this.

The fourteenth day. After being hove to for twelve hours, we again carried on for the land. It was blowing a moderate north-northwest gale with a high northerly sea. Clear till dawn, it then clouded over with fog banks.

Making the land, it was most important to get "sights" for position, but the conditions for observing the sun were most unfavourable. It was misty, the boat was jumping like a flea, shipping seas fore and aft, and there was no "limb" to the sun, so I had to observe the centre by guesswork. Astronomically, the limb is the edge of sun or moon. If blurred by cloud or fog, it cannot be accurately "brought down" to the horizon. The centre is the spot required, so when the limb is too blurred you bring the centre of the bright spot behind the clouds down to the horizon. By practice, and taking a series of "sights," you can obtain an average that has no bigger error than one minute of arc.

At 9:45 A.M. the sun's limb was clear, but it was so misty that I kept low in the boat to bring the horizon closer, and so a little clearer. The lateness of the hour, and the misty horizon, made a poor observation for longitude. At noon the sun's limb was blurred by a thick haze, so I observed the centre for latitude. Error in latitude throws the longitude out, more so when the latter is observed, as now, too near noon. I told Sir Ernest that I could not be sure of our position to ten miles, so he would not agree to my trying to weather the northwest end of South Georgia, for fear of missing it. We then steered a little more easterly, to make a landfall on the west coast.*

In some respects our condition had become worse. The last two days we had only brackish water from the stove-in "breaker" to drink. This seemed to add to our thirst. We dipped it through the bunghole, with the six-inch by one-inch tube provided for the purpose, and strained it with a piece of medicated gauze, to free it of sediment, dirt, and reindeer hair. One gill a man a day was all that could be spared. The hot milk at

---

* The whaling stations of South Georgia were located on the northeast coast. Shackleton decided to make for the uninhabited southwest coast rather than risk missing the island entirely because of poor visibility, the prevailing westerlies, and the ten-mile error factor.

138

night was stopped and hoosh was only made twice daily.

I think the others all suffered badly from thirst; for some reason it did not trouble me so much, though I would have liked a few hot toddies or a jug of cocoa. The situation had grown critical. If we had been driven off the land, or had not seen any ice, we should have been done for, unless we could have killed sea birds for their blood.

When short of water, keeping men wet with sea water compensates to a large extent. This, I think, applies to a normal or hot climate, where, the pores being open, the skin can "drink." We were wet all the time, but it did not appear to reduce our thirst, probably because the cold closed our pores.

Just before dark, eighty miles offshore, we saw a piece of kelp. We joyfully hailed it as a sign of nearness to the land, though it may have been borne by the current from the Shag Rocks—the mythical Aurora Islands to the westward.

All night we steered east-northeast, with a strong north-northwest breeze, recklessly burning inches of our precious candle. The seas came fast and merrily over us as usual, but we had a happy feeling that our worst troubles were over; we were nearly there.

At dawn on the fifteenth day, May 8, we saw some pieces of seaweed. Cape pigeons, albatross, mollyhawks, and the bobtailed birds grew numerous.

I looked anxiously for the sun. My navigation had been, perforce, so extraordinarily crude that a good landfall could hardly be looked for. The sky was overcast, and the weather misty and foggy, with a few clear intervals. Cross swells, and a heavy, confused, lumpy sea, made us wetter than usual, but a subdued joy and a species of quiet excitement held us, for we were making the land, and even hoped by dark to be on good solid earth once more, with beautiful clean water gurgling down our parched throats. We talked of how soon we should be at the whaling stations, with clean, dry clothes, and clean, dry beds to sleep in. Poor fools! We didn't know.

Fifteen miles offshore we saw the first shag. The sight of these birds is a guarantee that you are within fifteen miles of the land, as they hardly ever venture farther out.

By noon the fog had cleared, but heavy, ragged, low clouds were driving hard across from west-northwest, and still we had not sighted land.

Misty squalls at times obscured the view. Several patches of kelp were seen; and then, half an hour past noon, Macarty raised the cheerful cry, "Land ho!" There, right ahead, through a rift in the flying scud, our glad but salt-blurred eyes saw a towering black crag, with a lacework of snow around its flanks. One glimpse, and it was hidden again. We looked at each other with cheerful, foolish grins. The thoughts uppermost were: "We've done it. We'll get a drink tonight. In a week we'll get them off Elephant Island."

The land, Cape Demidov, the northern headland of King Haakon Sound, was ten miles distant when sighted. Wonderful to say, the landfall was quite correct, though we were a little astern through imperfect rating of my chronometer at Elephant Island.

Hove To

We had been exactly fourteen days on the passage from land to land.

An hour later the coast was visible to port and starboard. A desolate, forbidding coast, but that did not trouble us much.

As we drew inshore we passed close north of an area of huge "blind" rollers on an uncharted shoal. Norsemen call them "blinders." Ahead of us, and to the south, sudden great spouts of white and terrific roaring combers showed where the battle raged between the wild westerly swell and uncharted reefs off the coast.

By 3 P.M. we could see small patches of green and areas of yellow-brown tussock showing through the snow on Cape Demidov.

Sir Ernest considered it too dangerous to stand on when I told him King Haakon Sound was right ahead and Wilson Harbour to the north. The former lies open to the west, and it would have been madness to land, in the dark, with a heavy sea, on a beach we had never seen and which had never been properly charted.

Wilson Harbour would have been good, but it was to wind'ard, and against the heavy sea we could not make it.

After a fierce, stormy-looking sunset the wind hauled to west-southwest and blew a hard gale with rain, snow, sleet, and hail to give a bitter edge to our disappointment.

We stood off on the starboard tack till midnight, then hove to, eighteen miles offshore.

141

The heavy westerly swell increased. All night the *Caird* fell about in a very dangerous, lumpy, and confused sea, that seemed to run in on us from all directions, so that we sometimes shipped two seas over from opposite sides at the same time.

All night, even when hove to, with the reefed jib on the main, we had to bale and pump at very frequent intervals. It seemed to me that she was leaking badly besides shipping seas overall.

At daybreak on May 9 we were wallowing in a terribly heavy cross sea, with a mountainous westerly swell setting us in on the coast before the furious westerly gale then raging. We felt none too easy in our minds, for we knew the current was aiding the wind and sea in forcing us towards destruction.

All day we were stormed at in turns by rain, hail, sleet, and snow, and half the time our view was obscured by thick, driving, misty squalls that whipped the sea into lines of yeasty foam.

By noon the gale had risen to hurricane force, hauled to southwest, and was driving us, harder than ever, straight for that ironbound coast. We thought but did not say those words, so fateful to the seaman, "a lee shore."

Each time we were lifted high on a towering swell we anxiously searched the horizon to leeward for the break of an unknown reef or the dreaded coast. "Sea room, sea room, or a change of wind," was our mental prayer.

Dead reckoning was of slight use to give us our position in this hurricane, for the currents and tides on this coast, though fast and dangerous, are still unrecorded. All we knew was we were setting onshore.

We remained hove to till 2 P.M., when through a sudden rift in the storm-driven clouds we saw two high, jagged crags and a line of precipitous cliffs and glacier fronts on our lee quarter. We were being literally blown onshore—in the most dangerous and unknown part of the coast—the stretch between King Haakon Sound and Annenkov Island.

As we drove inshore it seemed that only three or four of the giant deep-sea swells separated us from the cliffs of destruction—the coast of death.

If we could have appreciated it, a magnificent, awe-inspiring scene lay before us.

The sky all torn, flying scud—the sea to wind'ard like surf on a shallow coast—one great roaring line of breaking seas behind another, till lost in spume, spindrift, and the fierce squalls that were feeding the seas. Mist from their flying tops cut off by the wind filled the great hollows between the swells. The ocean was everywhere covered by a gauzy tracery of foam with lines of yeasty froth, save where boiling white masses of breaking seas had left their mark on an acre of the surface.

On each sea the boat swept upward till she heeled before the droning fury of the hurricane, then fell staggering into the hollow, almost becalmed. Each sea, as it swept us closer in, galloped madly, with increasing fury, for the opposing cliffs, glaciers, and rocky points. It seemed but a few moments till it was thundering on the coast beneath icy uplands, great snow-clad peaks, and cloud-piercing crags.

It was the most awe-inspiring and dangerous position any of us had ever been in. It looked as though we were doomed—past the skill of man to save.

With infinite difficulty and danger of being washed overboard we got the reefed jib off the main, set it for'ard, set reefed lug and mizen, and with these large handkerchiefs endeavoured to claw offshore, praying to Heaven that the mast would stand it.

She gathered way, then crash! she struck an onrushing sea that swept her fore and aft even to the mastheads. While all baled and pumped for dear life, she seemed to stop, then again charged a galloping wall, of water, slam! like striking a stone wall with such force that the bow planks opened and lines of water spurted in from every seam, as she halted, trembling, and then leaped forward again. The strains, shocks, and blows were tremendous, threatening every minute to start her planking, while the bow seams opened and closed on every sea. Good boat! but how she stood it was a miracle of God's mercy.

While one steered, three worked the pump, one baled with the two-gallon hoosh pot, and the sixth stood by to relieve one of the others. Half the time he assisted with the small baler, and when opportunity offered, passed out a small lump of hoosh or some sea-damped lumps of sugar. Every hour we changed round to reduce fatigue.

As we looked at that hellish rock-bound coast, with its roaring breakers, we wondered, impersonally, at which spot our end was to come.

The thoughts of the others I did not know—mine were regret for having brought my diary and annoyance that no one would ever know we had got so far.

Frank Hurley and Sir Ernest Shackleton
at Ocean camp (Scott Polar Research Institute).

145

Ocean camp
(Scott Polar
Research Institute).

Bottom left: Young
emperor penguin chicks
(Scott Polar
Research Institute).

Bottom: Death stalks
the floes (National
Library of Australia).

A pinnacled glacier berg
(Scott Polar Research Institute).

Pulling up the boats below the cliffs of Elephant Island
(Scott Polar Research Institute).

The first meal on Elephant Island (Scott Polar Research Institute).

Tending to the invalids (Scott Polar Research Institute).

The rocky ramparts of Elephant Island
(Scott Polar Research Institute).

The *James Caird* being slid into the water
(National Library of Australia).

Glacier and mountains, South Georgia
(Scott Polar Research Institute).

Above left: The men left on
Elephant Island digging a shelter
(Scott Polar Research Institute).

Overleaf: South Georgia
(National Library of Australia).

Skinning seals on Elephant Island
(Scott Polar Research Institute).

Hut in which members of the expedition lived for four and one-half months (Scott Polar Research Institute).

Inaccessible mountain, the highest point of Elephant Island (Scott Polar Research Institute).

Members of the expedition on Elephant Island (Scott Polar Research Institute).

Arrival of the rescue ship off Elephant Island.
Note figures at left, signalling.
(Scott Polar Research Institute).

Saved! (Scott Polar Research Institute).

At intervals we lied, saying, "I think she'll clear it."

For three hours, our thirst almost forgotten, we looked Death square in the eye. It was not so much terrifying as chilling, especially in conjunction with the ceaseless rush of breaking seas over us.

Just then the land parallel to our course, and onto which we were being driven, receded slightly to the eastward, giving us a little more sea room.

Then just as it seemed we might draw clear, a new danger threatened. The mountain peak of Annenkov Island loomed menacingly close on the lee bow. We headed to wind'ard of it, but leeway and the heavy sea appeared to be carrying us on to its western point. We could have kept away and gone to leeward of it, but we dared not, with darkness coming on; besides the danger of the coast we were clearing, an eight-mile-long reef was marked on the chart, between Annenkov and South Georgia. We caught glimpses of it and others not charted and held on to wind'ard. Our chart, imperfect at best, was almost illegible from sea stains, and so was but a doubtful guide.

Darkness settled on six men driving a boat slamming at the seas and steadily baling death overboard. The pale snow-capped peak gleamed spectrally aloft, resting on black shades of cliffs and rocks, fringed by a roaring line of foaming breakers—white horses of the hurricane, whose pounding hooves we felt, in imagination, smashing our frail craft.

We peered under the clew of the sail and said encouragingly to each other, "She'll do it," even when we felt it most impossible. The island came so close that we had to crane our necks to look up at the peak.

At one time we were almost in the yeasty backwash of the surf; I believe that some eddy of the tide or current drove us clear.

Foot by foot we staggered and lurched drunkenly past the ravening black fangs of the rocky point. The moments became so tense that we feared even to speak—just held our breath or baled harder.

By 9 P.M. we knew we were safe. High, almost overhead it seemed, the great peak loomed mysteriously through the darkness. Right abeam, long pale fingers from the surf reached back—threatening but impotent —no longer did we fear them; every minute the clamorous roar on the rocky point became more faint with distance on the lee quarter.

Strangely, as soon as the worst danger was passed, the hurricane decreased rapidly. Half an hour later the wind came ahead from south-southwest.

We wore her round before the wind and stood back northwest, taking care to pass well to wind'ard of our enemy.

For nine hours we had fought at its height a hurricane so fierce that, as we heard later, a 500-ton steamer from Buenos Ayres to South Georgia had foundered in it with all hands, while we, by the grace of God, had pulled through in a twenty-two-foot boat. I doubt if any of us had ever experienced a fiercer blow than that from noon to 9 P.M.

After the boat was freed of water, the watch could handle her and keep her afloat. At midnight three men crawled below for three and a half hours' sleep. The other three got their sleep in the morning watch before sunrise. Now we had time to realize how bad our thirst was. The water finished, our mouths and tongues were so dry and swollen that we could only chew a few morsels of food.

At daybreak, all reefs shaken out, the *Caird* was doing her best to get us to a drink and the shelter of the nearest good bay to the north, before another gale came on. The wind backed to northwest and was falling, so we had to make for King Haakon Sound, the entrance to which lay nine miles ahead.

The sun shone at intervals on the snow-clad land, and indigo blue majestic rollers that topped up on the shoals, spouted white beacon warnings on the reefs, and hurled their loud shouting cohorts on the black spears of the rocky headlands. The ebb and flow of their strife could be heard five miles offshore.

Quoting from my navigation book: "All very thirsty and badly in need of sleep. Some of our people, in fact, seem just about played out. Macarty, Vincent, Crean, and I take turns at the two oars, sitting up on the deck trying to pull into the bay."

Breakfast was a sorry jest. We chewed, and with difficulty swallowed, a lump of hoosh the size of a hen's egg. Crean, crawling from his sleeping bag under the thwart, struck it with his shoulder. The pin that held the mast clamp in place must have worked upwards during the hurricane, till the point alone held. The slight shock from Crean's shoulder knocked it out. The clamp swung open, and the mast started to fall aft, but Macarty caught it and clamped and secured it with the pin. Happening then it was a trifling incident, but the pin had probably held in that precarious position all night. Had it fallen out in the hurricane, the mast would have snapped like a carrot, and no power on earth could have saved us. Providence had certainly held us in the hollow of His hand.

Soon after breakfast we passed between two headlands six miles apart, and by noon could see north of us two large glaciers which promised floating ice. For a while we steered towards this bay, but seeing that there was no shelter and we could not make it before dark, the course was resumed for King Haakon Sound.

By noon the wind had shifted to east and blew strong in our teeth right out of the sound. At the same time the tide was setting us to the south'ard. We lowered the sails; Crean and I pulled with the two oars, relieved at short intervals by Vincent and Macarty, as owing to the cramped position it was impossible to pull for long. The wind was too strong for us, and finding we were setting unpleasantly close to the breakers, we again set jib, mainsail, and thrice-accursed mizen, and so beat up against the wind.

We could make no pretence of eating a midday meal. We just longed for water.

For four hours we tacked, tacked, tacked, till we were sick of it. Although our boat was overballasted, she made little or no gain to wind'ard. We again got out the oars, this time to assist the sails, and by pulling to wind'ard only, counteracted the boat's griping, and so saved the drag of the rudder across her stern. Now, by dint of hard work, we gradually drew nearer to the strange, block-shaped rocks and islets that stretch, like a boom defence, across two-thirds of the entrance. We noted that at the head of the sound was a comparatively low, easy slope or saddle leading to the interior.

We speculated we could win our way by this on foot across South Georgia.

Still no floating ice to ease our thirst—the wind blew stronger. It looked as though we might, in the darkness, once more get driven out to sea.

Late in the afternoon we got up to patches and lines of kelp extending from the chain of rocky islets. Had it come to the worst, we could have moored the boat to the kelp for the night by seizing strand after strand of the long leathery, slippery plants, and, laying them together, formed a fine resilient cable. Darwin observed kelp reaching the surface in 100 fathoms. I have often seen it do so in eighty to ninety fathoms. This gives it a length of 600 feet—100 feet longer than the tallest tree in the world.

Evening drew on, and it was evident that without a change of wind we could not get our overburdened boat into the sound, and land that night. Then, through the gathering gloom, we saw to the south what looked like a cove with a possible landing behind a headland which broke the heaviest of the Southern Ocean swells.

We weathered its entrance, then turned and ran before the wind for 300 yards, closely searching the rocky shores for a possible landing. There was none. We were then abreast of the entrance to the cove, and, putting out the oars to steady her, we hauled to the wind on the port tack and passed between the rocks that stood off both headlands, leaving such a narrow passage that our oars fouled the kelp on both sides.

We then lowered the sail and pulled about sixty yards, between cliffs rising eighty feet high that flanked the tiny cove, until we came to the boulder beach at the head. It was now dark.

As we beached the boat in the surf at the southwest corner of the cove and jumped ashore, we fell down into pools of running water; kneeling, we lapped it up greedily.

Sir Ernest decided to get everything out of the boat to haul her clear of the water. He clambered about ten feet up the rocky face at the foot of the cliff on our starboard side, where I threw him a rope, which he made fast to hold the boat. In doing this, through stiffness and awkwardness from being so long cramped in the boat, he fell some way and hurt himself, but luckily sustained no serious injury. At this time the boat's stern swung against the rocks, unshipping the rudder and carrying away the lanyard that held it, so that in the darkness it was lost.

It seemed, in our exhausted condition, a terribly laborious and endless job unloading and clearing the boat of all gear. I well remember the sensations of misery and fatigue crawling along in water and darkness under the canvas covering of the boat, splashing cold and wet on hands and knees, passing stores up to Crean, who passed them to Sir Ernest. While Macarty and Vincent carried everything above reach of the waves, McNeish held the boat. This took up until 8 P.M., and we were continually falling, owing to our swollen and numbed feet and cramped feeling from lack of exercise in the boat.

Meantime Sir Ernest got the "Primus" going, and we had hot milk made from dried milk powder. This put fresh life into us, and we soon finished the work.

Then we had time for a meal. While the others cooked hoosh, I held the boat, hauling the painter taut and belaying it round a boulder. In spite of all efforts the boat bumped heavily in the surf on the boulders —we were too weakened to haul her clear—to such an extent that we expected her to be stove in every moment. We afterwards found the planks had chafed in places to the thinness of cardboard.

After a delicious feed of boiling hot hoosh cooked over the "Primus," Crean exploring returned across the eighty yards of boulders that separated us from the cliffs on the other side of the cove with the joyful news of a "cave." It is hard to realize what the word meant to us. Apart from the ineradicable schoolboy love of a cave, it sounded to us like a great dry, roomy dwelling with a steady floor, after the never-ending motion of the boat, the cold and wet, and sleeping on the ice floes. However, it proved to be merely an undercut face of the cliff, with huge fifteen-feet-long icicles hanging down in front, ready to impale an unwary visitor. When we saw it we rather damped Crean's enthusiasm; still, it served our purpose.

Stumbling, falling—our feet were numbed, yet sore, soft, and superficially frostbitten from sixteen days' soaking in cold sea water, and we had partly lost control of them—we shambled along with our sleeping bags and the least wet of our clothing. We must have looked a sorry, miserable crew. At least two were nearly "all in." Sir Ernest told me afterwards that he was convinced they would have died, had we been out in the boat another twenty-four hours. Still, we were not woebegone, but looking forward with weary joy to a sleep on stable land once more. On a sloping bed of dry shingle we laid our sodden sleeping bags and, crawling in, snuggled against each other for some degree of warmth.

This was 10 P.M. Sir Ernest took the first watch by the boat, and, with his usual unselfishness, kept three hours instead of one. Just after he had been relieved by Crean we heard a shout. Rushing and falling along the boulder beach, we found that an extra large sea surging the boat had torn out the boulder to which I had belayed the painter. Crean, hanging on, had been dragged into the surf up to his waist. We "tailed on" to the painter, and after some exertion managed to get her bows hard aground so that we could hold her. During our efforts a crosscurrent had taken the boat and us with it along the beach till we were only twenty yards from the cave. This was better. It was then 2 A.M. and there was no more sleep for us.

Three of us held the boat and, when a heavier swell rolled in, the other three hauled with us against the undertow. We made a hot drink of milk and at daybreak hoosh was served piping hot.

Then we set seriously to work to get the boat up the beach. The tide here rises only three feet, but at high water we hauled her as far up as we could, and then to lighten the boat stripped her of everything movable. We had not rope enough to rig a purchase, so we placed her two masts and the spare mast under her keel and worked her uphill. Boulders sticking up in our course hindered us, but by noon we had got her so far up that we felt easier, and had a good rest and feed. Then we got her on to a patch of shingle where, using the masts as rollers, we hauled her diagonally and zigzag up the incline, until we got her in safety on the tussocks. Had we been fit and strong, we could have got the boat up with an hour's hard work; as it was it took us from daylight to dark and exhausted us. Sir Ernest had decided that he would not risk taking the boat around South Georgia to the east coast in her cut-down condition.

After our crossing of South Georgia the *James Caird* was sent by Sir Ernest to England and landed in Liverpool. In the spring of 1920 I brought her from Liverpool to London in a truck attached to a passenger train. My friend Commander Stenhouse, captain of Shackleton's other ship the *Aurora*, came to assist me. Sir Ernest then lent her to the Middlesex Hospital, when students dragged her through the streets of London, collecting money for the hospital.

She was next taken to the Albert Hall, where Sir Ernest lectured for the hospital, and later I assisted him to transfer her to the roof of Selfridge's, where a small charge to see her was made for the same purpose.

In 1921, Shackleton having presented her to Mr. Rowett, she was taken to the latter's estate at Frant, where she was not improved, in her old age, by the exposure, so Mr. Rowett handed her over to Dulwich, Sir Ernest's and his old school, where she now is. [In 1967 the *James Caird* was presented to the National Maritime Museum in Greenwich.]

Looking back on this great boat journey, it seems certain that some of our men would have succumbed to the terrible protracted strain but for Shackleton. So great was his care of his people, that, to rough men, it seemed at times to have a touch of woman about it, even to the verge of fussiness.

If a man shivered more than usual, he would plunge his hand into the heart of the spare clothes bag for the least sodden pair of socks for him.

He seemed to keep a mental finger on each man's pulse. If he noted one with signs of the strain telling on him he would order hot milk and soon all would be swallowing the scalding, life-giving drink to the especial benefit of the man, all unaware, for whom it had been ordered.

At all times he inspired men with a feeling, often illogical, that, even if things got worse, he would devise some means of easing their hardships.

PART III

Crossing
South Georgia

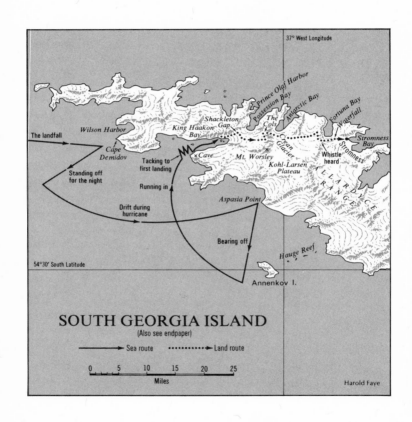

37° West Longitude

Prince Olaf Harbor
Possession Bay
Antarctic Bay
Fortuna Bay
Waterfall

Wilson Harbor

Shackleton Gap
King Haakon Bay
The Cols

The landfall

Cape Demidov

Tacking to first landing

Cave

Mt. Worsley

Crean Glacier

Whistle heard

Stromness Bay
Stromness

Standing off for the night

Running in

Kohl-Larsen Plateau

A L L A R D I C E   R A N G E

Drift during hurricane

Aspasia Point

Bearing off

Hauge Reef

54°30' South Latitude

Annenkov I.

SOUTH GEORGIA ISLAND
(Also see endpaper)

→ Sea route   ······▶ Land route

0   5   10   15   20   25
Miles

Harold Faye

I

Hoosh—what a joyous sound that word had for us. A corruption of a North American Indian word "hooch," meaning a drink, but now used in the form "hoosh" for a sloppy food that can be consumed by drinking—not necessarily by inhaling. Ours—carefully worked out by Sir Ernest and Colonel Beveridge, the British Army food expert—had been so well made that it defied scurvy. It was composed of lard, oatmeal, beef protein, vegetable protein, salt, and sugar. The result was heating, nourishing, and antiscorbutic, and it was invaluable. Made up in half-pound bricks for one man's meal, it had the consistency of a new cheese and a yellow-brown colour, but looked, when boiled with water, like thick pea soup.

In cooking, the aroma of this ambrosia rose as incense to the gods. Any one of us would cheerfully have murdered a Chinaman for a pound of it. With a gill of

"Johnnie Walker" it would have made a noble libation to Bacchus.

In hauling the boat over the rocks we had broken two masts, but did not grieve, as we had had enough sailing to last us a lifetime.

During the day I noticed a few dead tussock clumps, and in the dark, while the others cooked hoosh and slung the boat sails inside the icicles to screen our cave from the wind, I picked these and spread them on the sloping shingle floor of the cave. We turned our sleeping bags inside out and laid them on the boulders to catch some wintry gleams from the sun's rather watery eye. The result was that from being wet they had become comfortably damp. Hoosh this night was cooked over a real fire, made from the top sides of the boat and a few scraps of driftwood. How we revelled in the unaccustomed blaze! How luxurious we were, as we steamed our soaked extremities, rested our wearied bodies on sleeping bags and tussock grass, stuffed ourselves with hot, glorious hoosh, and smoked salt-sodden tobacco!

Exercise and a certain amount of drying were restoring the circulation and feeling to our feet, with the result that they began to burn painfully. We snuggled into our sleeping bags, pressed close against each other, feet to the fire, enjoying the comparative warmth and soft feeling of the tussock beneath us. The surf ten feet away made a soothing sound, punctuated at intervals by the dull boom of a glacier "calving" into the Sound. Twice we were startled by a ten-foot spike of ice falling with a crash on the boulders about ten feet away. Then sleep at last! Perfect and untroubled for four or five hours, when I awoke with my feet burning to such an extent that I thought my bag must be on fire, and, lifting my feet, asked Crean for an inspection. He reported all well, but not feeling content I asked Macarty the same question, with the same result. I dozed off, but waking in a few minutes asked Vincent if I was on fire. The reply again was no. By this time I had grown thoroughly unpopular and was reminded that other people had burning feet, so subsided into a tired-out sleep till daylight. When I turned out I found a hole about ten inches in diameter burnt in my sleeping bag and the heels of my socks burnt off! So I had something to complain of after all. What had happened was that the fire had caught the half-dried turf and tussocks that I had spread on the shingle, and these, smouldering, had eaten a way underneath to my bag, as was fitting. But it gives a good idea of the heat of our feet when one could not tell it from actual fire. Strange to say, my feet were uninjured—wet hide does not burn well.

Next day Shackleton, Crean, Macarty, and I explored inland, the others being still unfit to travel. We found a plateau with baby albatross on the nest. These nests are of turf and tussock, built up year after year till they are sometimes four feet high. They are quite in the open, and the parents sitting on the nests resemble, from a distance, a flock of scattered sheep on the hillside. They lay one and sometimes two eggs, six to seven inches long, on which cock and hen take turns at sitting. One often stands by the nest, making pointless remarks and noisily snapping its bill at intruders. The chick develops into a beautiful white ball of down,

175

like a huge powder puff, with a head at one end ornamented with beautiful, large, appealing eyes and a soft
beak, which it snaps impotently in imitation of its parents. These chicks give twelve or fourteen pounds of
delicious food, and were a godsend to our weakened
men. The first time I killed one I felt like a murderer,
the second time a little less bad, and after that I just
thought what a fine meal they would make, and what
a glorious feed the first had been. Skinned and cut up
into pieces, with half a pound of hoosh and a little
water, we simmered it over the tiny driftwood fire,
around which we crouched, holding various garments
to dry, while the smoke pursued us, on whichever side
of the fire we stood, and got into our eyes and noses
in the irritating way smoke from an open fire does.
When the dish was cooked we revelled in unwonted
gluttony—the delicious, white, well-flavoured, and
rich flesh was rendered even more piquant by the addition of the hoosh and a little salt, which we had
managed to save in a hermetically sealed tin. How we
stuffed! For once there was no stint. We even ate the
bones, as they were soft and juicy. A little of the liquor
that was left in the cooker cooled down into a fine, rich
jelly. It was far better than chicken broth for invalids,
and indeed, we needed it. After the feast, reclining
luxuriously on the tussock and sleeping bags, and con-
tentedly puffing foul-smelling cigarettes, the Boss and
I discussed making enough money to start another
expedition by taking some hundreds of baby albatross
and selling them to the epicures, gourmets, gour-
mands, gluttons, and whatnots of Europe and New
York at £50 a piece, quite ignoring the fact that there

is a regulation forbidding the killing of these chicks, which we were then transgressing under the sterner law of necessity. We were then a law unto ourselves, and looked it.

Crean and I were cooks—that is, Crean was a chef, I was a scullion. Poor Crean developed symptoms similar to snow blindness caused by the wood smoke. The Boss told him to wear his snow glasses, but he neglected to do so, and got worse, so I got temporary promotion.

At noon, standing on the beach with my sextant, I got the latitude by the sun. Our cave faced north, and the far side of the sound was four miles distant—too distant to interfere with bringing the sun down to the horizon. The result, $54°10'S$, proved we were where I had said—King Haakon Sound—and the German chart, the most accurate of South Georgia, was here one mile in error.

Our feet were now recovering, so that we could walk without stumbling, though we still shambled a bit, and whenever they got dry they felt as if burning.

Five P.M. —Supper of more albatross and hoosh; a brief smoke of now almost dry tobacco. This consisted of a few precious leaves that had been carefully picked out that day, from various parts of the boat into which they had been washed by the seas, during the boat journey.

As we smoked, leaning back against the rocky walls of the cave, we felt a great content. The hardest part of our task was completed, we were living in luxury and our only anxiety was about our shipmates in Elephant Island.

In The Cave

I was feeling drowsy when a loud crash right along-side startled all of us. We gingerly lifted the corner of the sail and peeped out. Two great spikes of ice had fallen from the "porch" and lay across our usual entrance. Looking up we saw that there was no more ice left directly overhead where the spikes had been, so we decided to stick to our original route of approach, but it was noteworthy next morning and from that time onward, that the "cave men's" entrances and exits were more hasty than dignified.

We pulled the sails tighter across the front of the cave, secured them with stones, and retired to what we looked on as our snug, but roomy and comfortable hostel. Steeply sloping shingle gave a dry base for the tussock, on which our now almost dry bags were luxuriously laid out. The sail left a gap between it and the rocky face, and the ocean was conveniently—almost inconveniently—near, just by our feet. Over the top of the sails we could see the black cliffs on the other side of the cave, with white uplands and banks of snow all along on top. We slept comfortably for about ten hours, except when disturbed by Crean's twisting and muffled groans from the pain of his eyes. Sir Ernest lost more sleep than we did, as he attended to Crean and put some adrenalin (suprarenal extract)—our cure for snow blindness—into his eyes. It sounded very quaint to hear Crean demurring like a fractious child, and Sir Ernest, like a worried parent, reproving him until he got him off to sleep. After this all was peace again until, at 2 A.M., Sir Ernest suddenly awoke us all by loudly shouting: "Look out, boys, look out! Hold on!" At the same moment he clutched me by the shoulder in his excitement. I sat up, looked around, and, seeing nothing of note, said: "What is it, Boss?" He said: "Look! It's just going to break on us," pointing to the black wall of cliff opposite, white-crested with snow, which he, dreaming of the boat journey and waking suddenly, imagined to be the great sea that broke over us six nights before we landed. After this quiet reigned until 8 A.M. We awoke, missing the familiar wash of the sea, but hearing a strange, crackling, whispering bumping that came and went, came and went, all the time. Looking out, we found our tiny cave full of glacier ice, heaving and cracking to a slight swell. A change of wind had brought it in and piled it on the beach and against our cave till the blocks were only prevented from piling on our feet by the bulging boat sails. This ice, of course, would prevent us from launching the boat for a day or two.

In the forenoon Crean, Macarty, and I went up on the plateau and brought down twelve young and one mature albatross, a very heavy load across rough country and snow. The grown albatross was an experiment we did not repeat, for, though well flavoured, he was very tough, and epicures, such as we then were, do not eat tough meat.

After lunch Shackleton and I set out to prospect for a possible route to the easy saddle we had seen the first day at the head of the sound. We traversed about five miles of very rough, hilly country, covered with close-packed tussock, snow, and swamp. Then we worked east along the boulder beach on the south side of the sound, passing a few herds and single sea elephants. Getting round one or two rocky points, we worked our way across two steep scree slopes, until we were brought up by an impassable glacier. From here we made a mental survey of the sound, and counted twelve glaciers falling into it. Sir Ernest named some of them, the first after myself. I am not sure that I remember which one now, but, in any case, there were enough to go round. Here Shackleton told me that he had decided, when he made the attempt to cross South Georgia, to take me, as he was sure of my endurance standing any strain. I squeezed his arm for this—we were sitting arm in arm on a tussock—for I felt proud and grateful.

On our way back we came across some spars and pieces of driftwood, which, if we got held here for the winter, meant firewood for us. These spars told tales of the loss of some gallant ships and men, probably off Cape Horn, drifted here before the nor'west gales. Sir Ernest picked up a pathetic little toy—a child's ship, one foot long. It may have told of tragedy, but at the least it was the minor tragedy of some child's lost treasure. Two miles from the cove we came across a seven-foot sea elephant. Not having a stick, I stunned him by hurling a small boulder on to his nose, then, turning butcher, took heart, liver, some flesh, and blubber for food and fuel. I took off my Burberry blouse, turned it inside out, and secured my share in it. Shackleton carried his over his shoulder, but we were equally hot and bloodstained when we arrived.

Sir Ernest, with his usual love of legpulling, said, with a twinkle in his eye: "We'll hide this stuff, go in and tell 'em you saved my life from a sea elephant that tore your blouse off and badly wounded you—to account for the blood." It was dark when we got back, after a heavy tramp of nine or ten miles. To our joy the hoosh was simmering. Of course our tale was not believed. When he said: "Guess what we've found," there were various guesses, from gold, diamonds, or ambergris to a whaler or a whaling station; but when we proudly produced blubber, liver, etc., there were cheers of joy, as all now knew that supplies would be assured for winter, if necessary.

Next day the cove was still filled with ice, but the boat was as ready as we could make her to proceed to the head of the sound, it being impossible to strike inland from the cove.

It blew a gale all day—snow and sleet squalls, great clouds wreathing around and over the mountains, and the wind whipping white the surface of the sound.

Next morning was our first fine day—a west wind ruffled the sparkling water outside the cove, starring it with white caps. Daybreak and hoosh—sleeping bags rolled up and cave abandoned. At eight we gave the dismantled *James Caird* a flying start down the steep beach, and, even as we launched her, saw an object bobbing in the surf—our wandering rudder, washed away to sea some days earlier. As Sir Ernest said: "With the whole broad Atlantic to choose from it came back and was cast at our feet." "Old Provvy" was looking out for us as the cove had been full of ice for three days. We discarded the steer oar, shipped the truant rudder, and went on our way rejoicing.

We pulled clear of the hospitable cove, then hoisted our sail to a fine, fair breeze, before which we ran about seven knots an hour up King Haakon Sound—

misnamed Bay on the chart. We felt really happy and excited. The weather was fine, the prospects looked good for us to cross South Georgia and get help for our shipmates on Elephant Island, and ahead of us was action—action always doubly inspiriting after enforced inactivity.

The saddle we saw from the boat the first day now showed up clearly, the only track to the interior. The hoarse, coughing, raucous roar of the bull sea elephants—pashas of the harems—told us food would be plentiful. Halfway up the sound we came to a band of kelp that stretched right across. Fearing hidden rocks I kept a sharp lookout from the bows, as Crean steered her through the kelp. Then we ran up towards a group of rocky islets at the head of the sound, but noticing a bold little bluff that rose islandlike from flats on the left, we made for that. Several herds of a score or more sea elephants were dotted along the flats. Running round two rocky little points we came to a long, sloping shingle beach. We lowered the sail, pulled in through a small surf, and beached the boat. Next we unloaded, carrying everything above high-water mark.

Just east of us was a marvellous pile of driftwood, covering half an acre, and piled from four to eight feet high in places. This was a graveyard of ships—woeful flotsam and jetsam—sport of the sea: lower masts, topmasts, a great mainyard, ships' timbers, bones of brave ships, and bones of brave men. Most of it had drifted a thousand miles from Cape Horn, some of it two thousand miles or more.

Swept before the westerly gales on to this wild South Georgian coast, the easterly current, by some strange freak of eddies, threw it up in this one spot— a sad tale of wasted human endeavour, of gallant seamen beaten by the remorseless sea. Piled in utter confusion lay beautifully carved figureheads, well-turned teak stanchions with brass caps, handrails clothed in canvas "coachwhipping" finished off with "Turks' heads"—the proud work of some natty, clever AB; cabin doors, broken skylights, teak scuttles, binnacle stands, boats' skids, gratings, headboards, barricoes, oars, and "harness casks." There the mighty roaring Southern Ocean, tiring of its sport, had cast them up contemptuously to rot, in grievous memory of proud, tall ships with lofty spars, of swift clippers, barques, barquentines, possibly even an old East Indiaman. Wreckage from schooners, sealers, whalers, poachers, pirates, and maybe even bits of a man-o'-war, lay around, for some of it may even have drifted there when Drake first battled round the Horn. "Some day, Skipper," said "Shacks," "you and I will come and dig here for old treasure, or perhaps sleep quietly with the other old seamen."

We selected the best rollers we could find and, placing them under the boat, soon worked her up on to the land. Five or six hours of strenuous toil, punctuated by hoosh, and we had got the boat upside down on shingle against a turf-covered rocky bank outcropping through the snow. With boulders, tussocks torn up by the roots, and turf, we closed the bows, stern, and bankside, and covered the remaining opening, away from the bank, with the mainsail, secured with stones.

Killing a young sea elephant, we made a combined sea-elephant-baby-albatross hoosh, which was pronounced A1 at Lloyd's. We had brought, by way of precaution and luxury, six baby albatross from Cave Camp to Peggotty Camp, as I named the upturned boat. We placed oars and boards from the wreckage on the thwarts till we formed a beautiful dry upper story to our bijou cottage, and, thoroughly tired out, slept all night the sleep of the conscienceless sailor, lulled by the soft, murmurous tones of the sea on the beach.

Next day, a sou'west gale blowing, with snow squalls, we completed Peggotty House by planting tussocks and moss over it till it looked like an Irish turfed hut, with the smoke of our blubber-driftwood fire pouring out of a gap we had left near the bows. We made this fire under the boat to dry everything, for there was so much salt from the boat journey in clothing and bedding that they absorbed moisture from the very damp air. We soon found the main effect was to spread a blubbery soot over everything in the house, including the lodgers. After nearly asphyxiating ourselves and making our eyes run rivulets, we put the fire out. Sir Ernest and I then prospected over the flat at the back of the camp to a huge glacier that, ploughing down, pushed a moraine over the flats. Skirting east along the glacier front and behind the "graveyard," we came to huge "snouts" of ice projecting over 200 yards of the beach. It was high tide, there was a swell running in, and, as the first wave receded, I ducked under a snout of ice projecting forty feet and weighing as many tons, and ran to the nook between two snouts. Sir Ernest followed, and we rushed past two more snouts, when he, always cautious, said: "Too risky, come back, Skipper," and we ran back in stages. We certainly wasted no time when under the snouts, for we could see ice masses of 50 to 100 tons lying on the beach, and, had one such fallen as we ran under, pancakes would have been useful commodities compared with us. Then we climbed cautiously up on the treacherous surface of the glacier for a quarter of a mile, traversing to the east, and prospected two miles farther on for a route to the saddle, from which we intended to attack the crossing of South Georgia.

When we returned we found "Chips," Macarty, and Vincent had completed a rough little sled to drag across on our journey and Crean had got the gear generally ready, including three blankets, for it was Sir Ernest's original intention to have taken blankets as far as we could for one night's sleep. After hoosh, feeling cold under the boat, we again lit a fire and turned in. We got up a comfortable warmth, but were nearly suffocated, and got sootier than ever before it went out. During the night the moon came out and Crean suddenly let out a shout, swearing he had seen a rat—a statement that we received with roars of derision. Later "Chips" also saw one. The derision this time was less pronounced, especially when we came to think of the fact that rats swarm on the east coast and might be expected near all this wreckage.

When we turned out it was stormy as usual, the wind from nor'-nor'west, with misty rain squalls and comparative warmth, causing the great glacier at the southeast corner of the sound to "calve" frequently with a noise like thunder.

After breakfast, noticing everybody was very dirty

and attacked by a sudden fit of cleanliness, I cleaned my hands, after repeated trials, by rubbing them with snow, till the dirt came off in rolls. I then performed on my face, and, when I judged it to be sufficiently clean, crawled under the boat and rejoined the others. No remark, however, was made of my beautiful clean appearance, which I put down to jealousy on their part, but found, later, was due to the fact that, so far from cleaning my face, I had but rubbed the soot, dirt, and blubber that coated it into a blacker, shinier surface, until I was aggressively dirty!

Another stormy day. It was significant that, for ten days since we landed, there had never been a fine enough day to essay a start for the crossing, and now our anxiety was great, as the moon was full, and without fine weather and a full moon together it would be impossible to cross.

King Haakon Sound is on the uninhabited west coast. The whaling stations were all on the east coast. The necessity for crossing for help, with winter on us, was the ever-present fear that our shipmates on Elephant Island might starve, before even Shackleton's feverish anxiety could save them, so we dared not wait for spring and the whalers. As we could not, with two enfeebled men, take our boat around South Georgia, there was nothing for it but the crossing.

The aspects of the situation and the conditions we should face in the tramp across were as follows:

South Georgia, under the British flag, lies ninety miles west-northwest and east-southeast, with a very irregular breadth up to thirty miles. The backbone of the island is the great Allardyce Range, averaging

5,000 feet in height and culminating in Mt. Paget, 9,200 feet. Several peaks rise to over 6,000 feet. Huge lateral ranges strike off at about right angles. The interior is a sheet of ice and snow some hundreds of feet thick except where rocky cliffs and peaks break through. It had never been crossed except where Possession Bay, on the east coast, was separated by the previously mentioned saddle, only six miles across from King Haakon Sound on the west coast. Thence three miles more would take you to Prinz Olaf Harbour. I tried to persuade Sir Ernest to make this journey—I knew it was no use volunteering to go myself; but he would not, for at that time, so far as we knew, the whaling station there was only kept on in the summer. We afterwards found that it was kept running all that winter, and has not since been closed.

Terrific gales scourge the coasts of this Ice-land of the South, and on the ranges and uplands the storm demons work their wild will and wreak their fury, baffled by the rocky masses and buttresses of the mountains, but gouging and carving ditches, valleys, and sheer appalling canyons in the great sheets of névé and ice around their flanks. The hell that reigns up there in heavy storms, the glee of the west gale fiends, the thunderous hate of the grim nor'wester, the pitiless evil snarl of the easterly gales, and the shrieks and howls of the southerly blizzards with ever oncoming battalions of quick-firing hail squalls, followed by snow squalls, blind a man or take away his senses. The wind fiends, thrown hissing, snarling, reverberating from crag to crag, from peak to precipice, hurtle revengefully on to the ice sheets, and clawing, biting, gouging, tear out great chunks and lumps of ice to hurl them volcanically aloft in cloud dust of ice and snow. What happens can only be imagined, for no man could live in some of the gales where we stood later, but a faint realization came to us as, with a thrill of awe at the force of Nature and the insignificance of man, we lay looking down into a wind-carved chasm 200 feet deep and broad, and 2,000 feet long.

This, with some glaciers, crevasses, treacherous frozen lakes, cornice-concealed precipices, and deceptively accelerating ice slopes, was the country that Shackleton proposed to cross, so we had to go warily —to pick a day of finest, fairest weather, and a full moon to guide our steps by night.

Meantime, the strain of waiting and anxiety for his men was telling on him. He was then more discouraged, worried, and nearer to depression than I had ever known him. He said to me one day: "I will never take another expedition, Skipper."

After breakfast on May 17 Shackleton and I set out for the pass to Possession Bay, aiming for the spot where the saddle before mentioned met the southeast flank of a noble-looking isolated peak about 4,000 feet high. After three hours' heavy tramping among huge boulders, thrown down from the peak, and soft deep snow, we arrived at the saddle, but could see nothing of the country, for a thick misty squall had come up. After waiting twenty minutes in vain for it to pass, and feeling half-frozen, we returned to Peggotty Camp.

The evening of Thursday, May 18, the weather was rapidly improving, and at last showed signs of being settled. Sir Ernest decided that, if it so continued, he,

Crean and I would start at 3 A.M. All was ready, and "Chips" had fixed sixteen two-inch brass screws in our boot soles, point down, eight on each foot. These were to give us a good grip on the country. "Chips" said they were all he had, but a carpenter is a strange bird—prolific as a *Daily Mail* Wyandotte. He can always go on producing screws and nails—speak to him kindly and he'll lay another in your hand.

We turned in early, full of hope, and slept soundly, but, disturbed once by an untuneful nasal diapason, I turned out and met Sir Ernest, whose anxiety had already brought him out twice. To our joy the moon was shining, and, as mendacious sailors say, "scoffing up the clouds." Anyway, they were disappearing.

Friday, 2 A.M. Fine clear weather and moon shining brilliantly. Sir Ernest said to me: "We'll get under way now, Skipper." Called all hands, cooked and ate our hoosh, leaving Peggotty Camp at 3 A.M., and by the bright light of the moon easily found our way, half an hour later, to the sled we had taken out the previous day for the first lap of our journey. Vincent, who had bad rheumatism and was still severely chafed from the boat journey, was left in camp. "Chips" and Macarty accompanied us as far as the sled, where Sir Ernest decided, on "Chips'" account, to send them back.

How sad we should have been at parting with simple honest Timothy Macarty, AB, had we known we should only see him once again for two days. He went down in the war, fighting his gun to the last—three short weeks after landing in England. A big, brave, smiling, golden-hearted merchant service Jack—we, his shipmates who truly learned his worth in that boat journey, are proud of his memory. I always felt that, no matter where we were or what exalted company we might have been in, if Timothy Macarty passed by he must be welcomed to a place of honour and given the best of everything, as befitted a brave man and one of Nature's gentlemen. At 4 A.M. we three breasted the steep slope to the saddle, but after dragging the sled for 300 yards we willingly abandoned it, with a redistribution of gear and loads as follows: Each of us had three days' food—hoosh, three biscuits, and two cakes of Streimer's nut food—slung in a Burberry sock around our neck. I had the forethought to put a spare pair of not very damp socks on my shoulders, where they dried slightly, and also served as a useful pad to my load. Sir Ernest then made as equal a division as possible of the following stores: "Primus," small nine-inch aluminium cooker, binoculars, small sledging compass, adze with the handle cut down to one foot to cut steps in the ice, and about ninety feet of Alpine rope. In addition I had a small piece of the German blueprint chart of South Georgia, and a small silver compass given to me five years before in Switzerland. The larger sledging compass cost five guineas—my little one, half a guinea; but at this work the little fellow won every time. As usual I navigated, and my procedure was at first to lay the "chart" and sledging compass on the snow together and take a bearing of a distant peak or bluff near our course, and then steer by it. This compass was a nuisance to read, caused us to stop, and delayed us, and I soon found that, holding my little compass in my hand, tilting it when near the proper bearing to stop it swinging, and standing still for two seconds, I could instantly read the bearing and go on. What the others carried I forget—I carried two compasses, binoculars, food, and the Alpine rope, besides the chronometer, with which I had navigated the boat. This was slung around my neck by lampwick, inside my sweater, to keep it warm. I remember this very well, because I was half-strangled with four cords and straps around my neck before I coiled the Alpine rope on top of all, as we had to leave our arms clear to use our "alpenstocks." These were five-foot laths off one of the sledges that were to have been used in the trans-Antarctic journey.

II

At first I had the worst load, but when we had to rope up four miles after starting, I had slightly the best of it.

Our clothing was, first a suit of what had been heavy Jaeger underwear. It was now, after five months' constant wear, rather light. Over this an ordinary pair of trousers—mine were a dress pair, about which Shackleton used to chaff me, as they were not quite fit for a ballroom! As a matter of fact any one of us would have been turned out of an East End doss house. We wore heavy Jaeger wool sweaters, with an eight-inch blanket patch-pocket across the bosom—very chic. This pocket contained an omnium-gatherum—our spoon (speaking individually), half a biscuit, our sweetheart's photo (still speaking individually), paper for cigarettes, etc., and who knows what besides! Over the aforesaid rig we had Burberrys instead of furs—a blouse and trousers fastened securely around neck, wrists, waist, and ankles, so that no air could get in. The Burberrys, being windproof, surrounded us with an invisible garment of warmed air, but, not being airtight, did not make us perspire as furs would have done.

Our footgear was a heavy pair of socks in felt-lined Shackleton boots, now much the worse for wear. On our heads we wore woollen "Balaclava helemets," and on our hands a pair of woollen mitts with loose overall Burberry mitts.

After abandoning the sledge the weather became misty, and at 5:30 we suddenly found ourselves close up to a strange deep pit in the glacier, or ice sheets, on to which we had unwittingly wandered. It was about 100 feet deep and faced uphill instead of down, so that we only just discovered it in time to save falling in. We tramped steadily on and upward, and reached the saddle about 6:15, making short halts every quarter of an hour, as Sir Ernest reckoned that was the best way of avoiding fatigue.

Half an hour later we reached the northeast slope of the saddle, whence, to our surprise, we saw through the scattering mists a great frozen lake, shining in the moon's rays below us, a little to the north of our course, which should have been east; but as the lake offered a tempting surface along its southern edge, and there appeared to be an easy slope down, we made for it. This lake puzzled us, for, though we were prepared to find a few tarns, we had expected nothing of this size. Soon after seven we found we were on a glacier, and Shackleton called a halt to discuss the situation; at the same time we had a cold snack of pemmican and biscuit, with two lumps of sugar and a handful of snow for a drink. Dawn to the northeast, and soon the rosy clouds of mist were lifting, and the lake lengthening. Presently we saw it stretching to the horizon. It was, in fact, no lake, but an arm of the sea —Possession Bay. As it was impossible to get along the coast there was nothing for it but to retrace our steps. We diverged to the left as we ascended, and gradually swung round until we were again steering east. About eight the sun rose—our spirits with it. It was vital to have fine weather, and everything looked promising. We were travelling over what appeared to be an undulating sheet of snow and ice, and, after crossing a gully, started a long steady ascent that lay across our course at right angles from the main range. The snow upland over which we were travelling steepened ahead of us to a great ridge, through which five rocky crags, or nunataks, reared up like giant fingers, with what looked like passes between each pair. The right-hand one being the lowest, Shackleton agreed to my proposal that we should try it. Away to our right the ice sheets continued up steadily through a great break in the main range, apparently an easy way, but some miles longer, and no certainty of what lay on the other side. It was a prospect of spacious grandeur, solitude, and the exquisite purity of Alpine scenery, clear atmosphere, blue skies, a few soft, fleecy clouds, and brilliant sunshine on the snow valleys and uplands, with black, upthrusting crags, and peak beyond peak of the great Allardyce Range, snow-clad and majestic, glittering like armed monarchs in the morning sun. The only sounds were the crunch of our feet through the snow, the soft swish of the rope—we were roped now, ready for crevasses—and an occasional alarming sudden hiss as an area of the snow around fell about eight inches with us. Every step we took we sank halfway to our knees. The ascent grew steeper. At each quarter of an hour, when we halted for a minute, we threw ourselves flat on our backs, spread-eagled, and, drawing in great draughts of air, took the most complete rest in the shortest possible time. Our bodies perspired, but our feet were cold and wet from the snow getting in through the worn-out Burberry uppers of our boots and melting as we marched. Towards noon we reached the "pass," but to our disappointment found, on looking over, precipices and icefalls, with no possible descent. Between us and the next gap were the precipitous flanks of a craggy peak, so down we had to go, and up again—another steep struggle to the next gap. Halfway up Sir Ernest ordered "grub." I remember on this occasion, although my appetite generally was so good as to be a byword, that I wanted no food except half a biscuit, two lumps of sugar, and a handful of snow. I think when men are doing an extra hard feat of endurance or work, the less they eat for a start, the better. Shackleton, ever watchful, was quite concerned for me, till I told him how well I felt.

We reached the second gap, and, looking over, found the descent as impossible as before. Again the sickening retreat of our hard-won climb, and another still steeper climb past the farther flank of the next peak. As we got up to the third gap, which was a ridge of ice between two peaks, we lost the sun behind the mountains, and immediately felt colder. We were about 4,000 feet above sea level. Thinking my feet were frostbitten, as their feeling was not yet normal after the boat journey, I took off my footgear at the next stop, but found my feet all right, though very cold. I wrung out my dripping socks, wiped and rubbed my feet well, and put on the dry socks from my shoulders, replacing them with the wet ones—to Shackleton's amused admiration. He took his usual paternal interest and praised my foresight. I bound up the tattered uppers of my boots so carefully that little or no snow got in, and on renewing the march, my feet were glowing pleasantly. Crean's boots were, I think, a little better than mine; but how Sir Ernest avoided frostbite, wearing leather boots, is a mystery. With his usual self-sacrifice he had given his own Shackleton boots to one of the men in the boat.

The third gap was a ridge of ice between two peaks, with a broken-up descent on the far side that might or might not have been possible. I wanted to try it, but Sir Ernest, with his usual caution, said "No," and very likely he was right; but we all felt "fed up" with our wearying search up and down, up and down, for a road through.

While writing this seven years after (almost), each step of that journey comes back clearly, and even now I again find myself counting our party—Shackleton, Crean, and I and—who was the other? Of course, there were only three, but it is strange that in mentally reviewing the crossing we should always think of a fourth, and then correct ourselves.

Down again and up again, this time obliquely, with

the object of examining a possible route to the left or farther north, by taking it in our zigzag.

On arriving at the end of this traverse across a very steep slope, we found our way checked by a great chasm, cut down into the snow and ice by the wind and gales blowing round the flank of the next peak. We approached the edge gingerly, and, lying down on the cornice, where it projected least, we peered over and down through the fading light into a gloomy gulf about 200 feet deep and broad and 2,000 feet long. Two battleships could have been hidden in it; but what impressed us most was the fearful force of the elements that had cut and chiselled it out, while we knew that, if a gale came on, we could live but an hour or so on these wind-threshed summits and uplands.

Zigzagging up to the right and cutting steps in the steep slope with the adze, we arrived at the fourth gap, a razorback of ice, as darkness came on.

A sea fog that had been creeping up behind us from the west now completely obscured all the country we had crossed, and it was impossible in the darkness to the east of this great ridge to see what the descent was like. We straddled the ridge, legs dangling, and debated the point, with mist wreaths drifting over and between us, but fortunately going no farther. Darkness in front, fog behind—there was not much choice; but from the third gap it had looked as though there might be a way down here, and finally "Shacks" said: "We'll try it." Cutting every step with the adze and keeping the rope taut between us, he led down for about 200 yards, the slope easing a little all the time. He halted, and we worked down and sat on the little ledge he had cut. In the darkness it was impossible to see whether the slope steepened to a precipice or eased out on to the level that seemed so dim and far below. It looked like the latter, so again he said: "We'll try it." Each coiling our share of the rope beneath us for chafing gear, I straddled behind Sir Ernest, holding his shoulder. Crean did the same to me, and so, locked together, we let go. I was never more scared in my life than for the first thirty seconds. The speed was terrific. I think we all gasped at that hair-raising shoot into darkness. Crean had hard work to prevent the short-handled adze coming round and cutting us. Then, to our joy, the slope curved out, and we shot into a bank of soft snow. We estimated we had shot down a mile in two or three minutes, and had lowered our altitude by two or three thousand feet. We stood up and shook hands—very pleased with ourselves—until we inspected our trousers! Bad enough before, they were in rags now. No more glissades! We really could not afford it.

Probably our greatest risk had been that of starting an avalanche down the slope with us, which would have been unpleasant, to say the least. In any case we thought it better to move a little way out before cooking the hoosh.

Crean attended to the "Primus." Sir Ernest filled the cooker with packed snow, and I dug a two-foot pit in the snow in which the "Primus" was placed, and lit, to prevent it being blown out by a moderate, but piercingly cold, wind that had just started down from the main range.

The "Primus" flickered and flared, so Crean and I

lay over the hole, keeping the eddying gusts away. As soon as the snow melted a little more was put in to make enough liquid, and the hoosh was stirred in. I lay round the hole and Crean crouched over it, protecting and stirring, while we awaited impatiently the verdict of our chef—"she's biling, bhoys!" Up came the cooker and "Primus," which latter the wind promptly put out, while we three lay round the cooker and dipped our spoons—we had no mugs—one, two, three, one, two, three, in turn. It was the only way we could "whack out," and was an equitable arrangement, though Shackleton chaffingly accused Crean of having the biggest spoon, and he replied: "Holy smoke, look at the Skipper's mouth!" So I took advantage of the discussion to take another spoonful. The hoosh was splendid. Boiling hot, the one, two, three just gave it time to cool slightly, though we had trained mouths, gullets, and stomachs until we could have swallowed food at almost boiling point, and so we got an extra degree of warmth into chilled and shivering bodies. After scraping the pot we resumed our march, and were soon warm again, going with the wind, which was now falling light. Through the darkness we could see two great rocky bluffs on our right, running back to a ridge of rocky spikes and needles, and flanked by seracs and icefalls that came nearly to a head on our eastern course. These forced us a little to the left, but not too much, for we knew, by what we had seen from the ridge before dark, that on that side were dangerous glaciers, crevasses, and ice cliffs. So we cautiously worked our way in the dark up an easy grade, along what might be described as a narrow terrace of the ice sheet, that sloped in two directions—towards us, and to the sea on our left, where we could faintly make out Antarctic Bay.

Now a faint, luminous glow showed behind the spikes and rocky needles of the ridge to the southeast, and we knew our dear old friend, the moon, had not forgotten us. Behind the mountains she began to rise upwards and towards our left—the east, for in high latitudes it is very noticeable how a celestial object, on the same side of the equator, moves when rising—first towards the east (instead of away from it) and then towards the equator. Soon we saw a tiny arc of silver at the bottom of a gorge, showing at the next gap a little larger, and so, playing hide-and-seek, she inclined upwards until she cleared the last pillar of rock, emerging clear, full, radiant, and silver, to gladden our hearts and guide our footsteps with her kindly light. It was seven o'clock. We cleared the threatening area of crevasses and icefalls, and steadily ascended a long, sloping upland that stretched about seven miles ahead, with a huge dome-shaped rock, breaking through the icesheet on the sky line, for a guide.

Most of the way we had been sinking into the snow, often to our knees, which, with pulling our feet out again, made tramping a weariness. Now, to our relief, the surface got so firm that we seldom sank over our ankles, and, guided by the moon gleaming on them, we made for every hard patch that we could see ahead. Sometimes we would go along for over a hundred yards without sinking in at all, and laughed and shouted with joy. We had been tramping for sixteen hours. Sir Ernest now made the halts about every twenty minutes, and, as before, we spread-eagled on our backs for two minutes' rest.

At eleven, near the great domed rock, we made hoosh; but, the air being almost calm, a tiny pit in the snow was enough to protect the "Primus" flame.

At midnight we were at the top, and looking down a long slope bearing a little to the left to a large, open bay. It was difficult to judge our speed and the distance we had made good, and Shackleton fearing we might overshoot Stromness Bay whaling station, which would have been fatal, we decided to make down the northeast slope. The easy descent lured us on. It was grand, swinging on with only an occasional check, though the freer striding chafed the inside of our thighs, previously irritated with constant wettings from salt water, etc., until they were raw and bleeding.

By 2 A.M. we had come down so far that we could see some small rocky islets in the bay beneath us, and we discussed whether or not they could be the Blenheim Rocks, in Stromness Bay. Suddenly we found ourselves in a crevassed area, so we knew we were approaching the breaking-off edge of some glacier. As there was no such glacier in Stromness Bay we must have turned too soon towards the sea. Shackleton said: "We must turn back for a while," and we cautiously picked our way clear of the crevasses. Wearily and mechanically we retraced our footsteps upward for nearly a mile, then gradually curved off to the left, as we had done the previous morning from Possession Bay. The slope to the southeast became very steep, and I think this was the weariest part of the whole journey, partly, no doubt, from the hopeless feeling at having to retrace our steps and climb again to previously hard-won heights.

This was not to be wondered at. As the interior was unknown there was no chart of it, and recognition of the bits of the coast we could see was difficult by moonlight.

I was roped in the rear at this time, and noticed the rope so slack several times that I had difficult to avoid treading on it, and once, in fact, did so. This is irritating to the others in ordinary mountaineering, but with fatigued men it is almost more than they can bear if it happens often, and, following the example of our leader, we all did our utmost to help and consider each other and avoid any cause of annoyance, however trivial. Responding to Shackleton's unselfishness, teamwork was pulling us through. Although Crean and I had several times asked him to let us take the lead for a while, he would not, but led the whole journey, though it was certainly more exhausting breaking the trail, and I thought I could see it telling on him, yet he kept as cheery as ever. In normal times he would sometimes be irritable, but never when things were going badly and we were "up against it."

The slope up which we were going got very steep.

We were making for the only opening in a ridge of rocky mountains that lay athwart our course. This reminded one of the gap left when a tooth has been drawn. The snow ran up into and through it.

About 5 A.M. we reached the lower flank of the great buttress of rock on the right, and feeling woefully sleepy and weary we lay our three sticks across a corner in the rocks, sat on them, all three snuggling together for warmth, and leaning back against the rock. Crean and I fell asleep instantly. Shackleton, with his unselfishness and care of his men, kept awake, fearing if we all slept we should never awaken again. This very prevalent belief is, however, partly a fallacy; for with men in hard condition, and not underfed or exhausted to the point of using up their reserve strength, instances have often occurred of their sleeping in the snow without any bad effects, and I do not think, in our case, any harm would have resulted. On Shackleton's first expedition a young New Zealander lost his way in a blizzard, without extra clothing, and slept in the snow for twenty-four hours without harm.

After we had slept for ten minutes, in Shackleton's words, "I woke them and told them they had been asleep for half an hour and the moral effect of my deception did them as much good as if they had been." I certainly felt wonderfully refreshed.

The slope grew steeper still, and we struggled up it until just after six o'clock, when we reached the gap.

III

In a tiny terrace of snow we dug a hole and started the "Primus." While Crean cooked hoosh, Sir Ernest and I unroped, worked our way up to a better point of vantage, and looked for the best course. It was a clear, calm, lovely morning—the moon, her good work done, paling in the west—the dawn breaking early at our altitude, probably well over 4,000 feet.

Though dark beneath us, the panorama lay clear. Almost straight below were the dark waters of Fortuna Bay, with a great valley at the head, half filled with a mighty glacier that swept round the mountains with a noble curve, and was fed by another glacier that broke, farther south, through the ridge on which we were standing; so there seemed to be no road there. Beyond the valley was another transverse ridge, much lower than the one we were on, and beyond that some glimpses of the water of Stromness Bay—our goal. Sir Ernest recognized a remarkable Z-shaped stratification of the great rocky face on the far side of Stromness Bay, and we felt safe. No fear of overshooting our mark now, or losing our way.

Immediately in front of us the slope was precipitous. It went off, so far as we could tell, into a sheer cliff; but to the right it looked as though there was a possible descent. It seemed too good to be true, and I said so, quite solemnly, to Sir Ernest. We felt happy now we could see the end of our journey.

A yell from Crean: "Hoosh!" We hurried down and told him the good news.

We spooned our hoosh, one, two, three, out of the cooker, had two lumps of sugar each, and longed for cigarettes.

Sir Ernest asked me for the time. It was 6:55. He said: "We'll listen for the whaling station's whistle." Sure enough at seven, through the still morning air came the welcome sound of the turn-to whistles of the whaling station—the first sound we had heard of civilization for eighteen months.

As Sir Ernest said: "Never did music sound so sweet to our ears as that whistle."

For the second time on the journey we shook hands, and I could not refrain from yelling, "Yoicks! Tallyho!"

The oil in the "Primus" was finished. We threw it away—a slight lightening of our load. Everything we could get rid of was a help, by freeing our arms and hands for difficult ascents and descents, or saving something dangling round one's neck or shoulders.

Bearing to the right we made our way for half a mile downward and across a fairly sharp slope, which steepened gradually to a dangerous angle.

Generally Shackleton was cautious, sometimes too much so, I, perhaps, not enough; but now, when the slope looked so bad, I said it looked as though we would have to turn back and find a better way down; he said: "No, we'll try it." I think he felt we were drawing near the end of our tether, and it was now or never.

Keeping the rope taut between us he cut steps with the adze diagonally across the ice slope. For 100 yards it was touch and go—every lump of ice that started down gave one bump on the slope, and then off into space. A single slip from one of us would have meant the end of all three.

Past the danger point was a steep slope, down which steps had to be cut for a short distance. Crean at the back and I in the middle "anchored" at each step until Shackleton had cut the next. Presently we found ourselves on a slope that was faced with an inch or less of ice. The slope seemed too steep to hold snow, but it had probably been plastered and packed against the mountain face by heavy gales. The surface had then been melted by the summer sun, and frozen at night till it all held together.

Sir Ernest, lying flat on his back on the slope, eased himself down till he sat on one heel. Raising the other in the air at full length, he crashed it down through the inch of ice, forming a heel rest. Then, lowering himself on to that heel, he repeated the performance with the other, while we did the same and kept the rope taut. The second or third man's heel crashing into the same hole made it so large that it was easy for the rear man, a big, strong fellow like Crean, to hold the party safely. Now we made rapid and fairly easy progress down, not having to cut steps. We were walking downhill, lying flat on our backs. So steep was it that we felt an unreasonable fear, whenever we lifted our heads off the snow, that we would fall outwards and down.

For about a thousand feet we came down so, till the slope eased and we came on rocky gradients and ravines among the snow. Then across low hills, all rocks, potholes, and ravines, covered with snow. At last we got clear of this and on to the shore—fifteen minutes' splendid tramping over a level beach. From here we could look up and see a faint, thin line like a spider's, zigzagging in places—our tracks on the incredible face we had descended.

We passed several inquisitive gentoo penguins, like little Charlie Chaplins, and many sea elephants, until we came to the front of the great glacier which, fortunately, did not quite reach the sea.

There were long, gravelly flats, debris of the glacier, almost like quicksands, in which we sank halfway to our knees. The going was good for half a mile along the beach at the head of Fortuna Bay. Here we saw reindeer tracks and a dead sea elephant—shot by some "sportsman." Then, past some low cliff, and over rough country, we made our way inland. As we ascended the going became better, and now we looked for the best way into Stromness Bay, a big, forked sound with three whaling stations—Husvik, Stromness, and Leith—all run by Norwegians, although Leith station is owned by Lord Salvesen. Leith and Stromness were nearer, but the question was, which was the easier to get to. Sir Ernest decided for Stromness, so we bore a little farther to the right.

Soon we were going along in great style, when suddenly Crean fell through up to his middle in ice water! We were crossing a lake without knowing it. We pulled him out, and hurriedly, but gingerly, made our way to the nearest raised surface.

After this, about eleven, we had a biscuit, some Streimer's nut food, three or four lumps of sugar, and some snow. Crean was a bit cold, but otherwise none the worse for his ducking.

On again up rough country, till finally, at 1:15, we were standing on a 3,000-foot summit, looking down on to Stromness Bay, with two whalers steaming across it, looking like tiny insects on the water. We could also see part of the whaling station. I yelled and waved against the skyline, but, of course, no one saw or heard. We shook hands for the third time. It was cloudy now, with a moderate southerly wind.

There was a very steep slope down towards the station, and I wanted to take it; but Sir Ernest thought it too steep, so we bore to the left down a valley.

Six years later, to the month, I came down that slope with a crouching glissade, for 500 feet, ploughing through soft, deep snow. It was very steep, but quite workable. This shows the amount of extra distance we had to travel, owing to our complete ignorance of the configuration of the country, of which the chart gave no indication.

The little valley down which we were travelling got steeper and narrower, until we were forced to tramp along in the stream of icy water, in the middle sometimes knee-deep. I remember that it seemed a great hardship to us to be doing the last lap in this beastly cold water.

Presently the ravine ceased. There was a precipice and a waterfall across our course, and the sides of the ravine were like walls. Unless we went a mile back up the stream there was no way on except down the waterfall—about fifty feet high.

We looked at it and then at each other—frankly we did not like it, but we liked still less the idea of going back up that stream. There was no place to make the rope fast, but the solid rock on which we were standing had a slight bulge upwards, and at the back went down to a hollow.

We hung the rope down the waterfall, leading it over the bulge and down to the hollow, where there was a fathom left. This I bunched up and stamped into the rock as much as I could. Then we threw the adze and the pot down on to the rocks below. It was quite easy to hold the rope over the rough rock, and I suggested to Sir Ernest that, as I was the lightest, I should come down last, and they could catch me if the rope slipped. He went first in the waterfall, slid down all right, and stood on the rocks on one side; Crean next, and stood on the other side. Next I eased myself over gingerly and then, in sailor fashion, slid rapidly down so as to put no weight on the rope until just before I reached their outstretched hands, then checked hard, expecting the rope to come with me as they caught me. To my surprise it held, and then a strange thing happened.

The three of us tugged and hauled on that rope, but

could not dislodge it, though it only lay over the rock and was not made fast to anything. It might have been frozen; anyway, we left it there, and picking up the cooker and the adze went on down the rocks till we reached snow-covered hills, over which we travelled for half a mile, and then got to some frozen marshy flats very slippery with ice. Here, almost at the end of our journey, we nearly had an accident. The two-inch screws that we had in our boot soles at the start had, in the course of our thirty-six hours' strenuous tramp, worn down till they were flush with the leather and useless, so we slipped about, and, being tired, fell heavily several times, which shook us up badly and annoyed us very much, as we considered our troubles should be over. Crean fell right on the adze blade and narrowly missed cutting himself dangerously. As it was he cut some of his clothing. I think the adze was then thrown away.

Now a few hundred yards brought us to the longed-for station. No one had seen us.

Just beyond this I tried to adjust my rags. Sir Ernest loved to tell the tale against me, that I said: "Boss, there might be women here." Sir Ernest: "What of it?" I: "Well, look at us, but I'm all right." Sir Ernest: "Oh, you're all right? How's that?" And he would say: "Worsley produced three large safety pins. I asked for one, and he said, 'Not on your life,' and proceeded to pin himself together; but when Crean and I inspected the result we decided he had only drawn attention to his own deficiencies."

Fortunately there were no ladies, still, we were a terrible-looking trio of scarecrows, but had got so used to ourselves that we did not mind. Ragged, filthy, and evil-smelling; hair and beards long and matted with soot and blubber; unwashed for three months, and no bath nor change of clothing for seven months. Fortunately we had no vermin.

It was 3 P.M. Coming round the first building we met a Norwegian, wheeling a barrow. Sir Ernest asked him where Captain Sorlee was. He stared at us in amazement, grunted, and went on.

Next we met two Norwegian lads of seventeen or eighteen. I think they thought we were the devil; anyway, they bolted.

We went on to Sorlee's house and met a foreman. Sir Ernest asked him for Captain Sorlee. He said: "What do you want?" Shackleton said: "I want to see him, I know him." The man went inside and told Sorlee: "There are three funny-looking men outside, they say they know you." Sorlee came out and Shackleton said: "Do you know me, Sorlee?" Sorlee said: "No." Then I said: "Do you know me?" He looked at me and said emphatically "No," and evidently did not want to! When Shackleton told him we had lost our ship and crossed the island, Sorlee almost dragged us in. In the porch we, feeling ashamed of our state, took off our boots and some of our outer clothing.

Sir Ernest, to be polite, said to Sorlee: "I'm afraid we smell." But he replied: "That doesn't matter, we're used to it on a whaling station!"

By magic a civilized afternoon tea appeared, and while we ate cake, bread, and jam, and scones, and drank coffee, we exchanged news with Sorlee, telling him bits of our adventures, and he telling of the Great

War to three Rip Van Winkles, who listened in amazement to what had happened.

Sir Ernest asked Sorlee to take our photographs, but unfortunately he had no film, so the world lost a picture of its three dirtiest men.

By this time Sorlee's steward had got the first hot bath ready, and while one bathed, another shaved himself. We stripped and compared results. All of us were chafed to the likeness of a raw beefsteak down our thighs and showed other signs of what we had been through. We expected to take a fortnight to heal, but such was our hard, healthy condition that in three or four days there was nothing to show.

The luxury of that glorious bath! It seemed worth while to have gone through what we had for the bath alone, as we soaped and washed and relaxed our fatigued and stiffened limbs in the hot, clean water, and afterwards got into clean underclothes and suits.

We had been going hard for thirty-six hours, 20 or 22 statute miles in a straight line, but which our devious course had probably doubled. The exertion of climbing in soft snow in our rig, cutting steps in ice, our feet not in the best condition, and much of our work at an altitude of over 4,000 feet, was equal to 3 1/2 miles an hour. This would make our exertion equal to well over 120 miles in normal conditions.

Captain Sorlee, our Norwegian host, a generous and sympathetic man, could not do enough for us. He was manager of the Tonsberg Whaling Company, and put the whole resources of the place at our disposal, lending Sir Ernest a steam whaler to get our three men from King Haakon Sound.

His steward, in particular, looked after us like a hen with three chicks, and evidently considered us his own peculiar property.

Before bathing I saw myself in the mirror, and found the reason for Sorlee's extra contempt of my looks. When—three days before, living under the boat —I had attempted to wash my face with snow I had, as I have said, merely rubbed soot and blubber into a sort of polished paste. The result was awful.

After the bath, shave, and clothes, feeling clean, proud, and happy, we had a royal dinner with our host.

Soon after I went on board the whaler *Samson,* to go back to King Haakon Sound and get the three men we had left under the boat. As I lay down to sleep in a comfortable bunk, with clean sheets, the whaler was steaming out of Stromness Bay. It was nine o'clock, and the last sound I heard was a rising southeast gale, which blew all night, beginning five or six hours after we had got through. Had we been crossing that night nothing could have saved us. The Norwegians afterwards told us there was never another day during the rest of the winter that was fine enough for us to have lived through on top of the mountains. Providence had certainly looked after us.

Three or four weeks afterwards Sir Ernest and I, comparing notes, found that we each had a strange feeling that there had been a fourth in our party, and Crean afterwards confessed to the same feeling.

I awoke after eleven hours' refreshing sleep, feeling fit for anything, to find we had rounded the western point of South Georgia, and were approaching the entrance to King Haakon Sound. Warning the captain of a reef we had observed from the boat nearly three miles off the northern headland, I went down for a huge breakfast. I had just finished, and feeling a heavy shock ran on deck, to see that we had found the end of the reef all right. Fortunately we had only taken one bump over it, and sustained no particular damage. Soon after we passed our Cave Cove and Albatross Plateau, and, heading up the sound in clear weather, sighted the upturned boat. A blast from the whistle brought our men crawling out hastily.

We threw the pram over. The captain, an AB, and I jumped in and were ashore in three minutes. I was dressed in a new Norwegian suit, pockets stuffed with pipes, tobacco, cigarettes, and matches. Coming up just behind the Norwegians, who were welcoming our men, I heard Macarty say disappointedly: "Well, we thought the Skipper would have come back, anyway." I said: "Well, I *am* here," and they stared. Clean and shaved, they had taken me for a Norwegian! They fell on the smokes like tigers, and were happy.

Then we all ran the *James Caird* down to the beach, launched her, and soon had her and the men on board, steaming back full speed for Stromness.

Late that night the southeast gale had increased so, with such thick weather, that even the whaling captain could not find his way in, and it was next day before we found ourselves in Grytviken, twenty miles down the coast.

Sir Ernest, meantime, had got the whaler *Southern Sky* for us to get the men off Elephant Island. In the afternoon we landed the boat at Leith. The Norwegians would not let us put a hand to her, and every man on the place claimed the honour of helping to haul her up to the wharf. I think Shackleton must have felt it one of the proudest moments. The amazed admiration of these sailor descendants of Vikings was so spontaneous and hearty that it was quite affecting.

In the evening the manager told Sir Ernest that a number of old captains and sailors wished to speak to and shake hands with him and us. We went into a large, low room, full of captains and mates and sailors, and hazy with tobacco smoke. Three or four white-haired veterans of the sea came forward; one spoke in Norse, and the manager translated. He said he had been at sea over forty years; that he knew this stormy Southern Ocean intimately, from South Georgia to Cape Horn, from Elephant Island to the South Orkneys, and that never had he heard of such a wonderful feat of daring seamanship as bringing the twenty-two-foot open boat from Elephant Island to South Georgia, and then to crown it, tramping across the ice and snow and rocky heights of the interior, and that he felt it an honour to meet and shake hands with Sir Ernest and his comrades. He finished with a dramatic gesture:

"These are men!"

All the seamen present then came forward and solemnly shook hands with us in turn. Coming from brother seamen, men of our own cloth and members of a great seafaring race like the Norwegians, this was a wonderful tribute, and one of which we all felt proud.

Next morning, May 23, Sir Ernest having made arrangements for Macarty, McNeish, and Vincent to return to England in the next steamer, he, Crean and I started from Husvik station, Stromness Bay, in the whaler *Southern Sky* (Captain Thom), with our decks nearly awash, for we had to carry enough coal to take us to Elephant Island and back to the Falklands.

Shackleton's aim was the rescue of the men on Elephant Island and during the next hundred days he, Crean, and I fought against the elements and every kind of difficulty to effect this purpose.

We spent all that winter in four attempts in different vessels. Some people thought that Shackleton was mad to take small, frail craft far south and into the pack in winter time, but his anxiety about his men was so terrible that it would not let him rest. During those hundred days he passed through hell. It has always been a source of satisfaction to me that my irrepressible optimism sometimes afforded him a target for chaff and lightened his burden through those days of storm and adversity. But the lines on his face became furrows and his thick, wavy hair showed streaks of grey.

In the *Southern Sky* we reached to within sixty miles of Elephant Island but were forced back by pack ice, snowstorms and shortage of coal. We returned to the Falkland Islands where Shackleton wired to Lady Shackleton and the King the news of our arrival and the plight of his men on Elephant Island. His Majesty replied, "Rejoice to hear of your safe arrival in the Falkland Islands and trust your comrades on Elephant Island may soon be rescued. George R.I."

The second attempt was made in the trawler *Institutio Pesca, No. 1,* which was generously lent to Shackleton by the Uruguayan Government. In this vessel we reached to within eighteen miles of the camp on Elephant Island, but were again driven back by the accursed pack. It lay closely packed between us and the island and was rising and falling on the northwest swell. If we had pushed the unprotected trawler into this ice she would have crumpled up like a kerosene tin before we had covered a quarter of the distance. We returned to Port Stanley with our bunkers almost empty.

From the Falkland Islands we went to Punta Arenas in the Magellan Straits. The British residents there and the Chileans very generously subscribed £1,500 which enabled Shackleton to charter and fit out the auxiliary schooner *Emma*. She was seventy feet long on the water line. I have commanded small sailing craft in some of the stormiest seas in the world, but that little schooner—with her forty-foot main boom, trying to take charge—flogging her way south from Cape Horn to the pack ice in the dead of winter, beat them all. We shipped a splendid, cheery little Chilean, Lieutenant Leon Aguirre, whose equipment was an oilskin coat, sea boots, and a guitar. Six men of six nationalities also signed on. One was from the Republic of Andorra and another had just served a year in gaol for seal poaching. He was a fine sailor.

That time we met the pack and entered it, one hundred miles north of Elephant Island. The auxiliary engine broke down, we received heavy blows from the heaving ice and after sustaining some damage were forced to retreat. We were glad to escape, for not only would we have lost the vessel and our lives if we had forced farther into the ice, but we would have delayed the rescue of the men who were awaiting us.

For the fourth attempt the Chilean Government came nobly to the rescue. They lent Shackleton the little steamer *Yelcho*. At the start we had a welcome change—fine weather from Cape Horn. But then we had to grope our way through fog and ice to the north-west breaker off Elephant Island. Finally we found the camp.

As I manoeuvred the *Yelcho* between stranded bergs and hidden reefs, Shackleton peered through his binoculars with painful anxiety. I heard his strained tones as he counted the figures that were crawling out from under the upturned boat. "Two—five—seven—" and then an exultant shout, "They're all there, Skipper. They are all safe!" His face lit up and years seemed to fall off his age. We three solemnly shook hands as if we were taking part in some ritual.

In three-quarters of an hour we were steaming back full speed for Cape Horn with every man safe on board. It was splendid to share their happiness and enthusiastic outlook. Shackleton was like an obnoxiously conceited but devoted parent with his offspring gathered round him. I felt like an experienced man of the world explaining to poor primitive people what they would see in civilization and what was happening in the world.

They had had a terrible time, waiting as patiently as they could in their miserable abode and hoping against hope that the boat had not foundered with us. Frank Wild's cheeriness had kept them up. Every morning he used to shout, "Lash up and stow! Roll up your bags, boys, the Boss may come today." Shackleton had every right to be proud, for it was his boast that he had never lost a life in any party that he was in charge of.

Very soon after the rescue all our fellows were taking their part in the Great War. Six months later our finest AB, Timothy Macarty, went down in his ship, fighting his gun to the last.

Six years later when looking at Shackleton's grave and the cairn which we, his comrades, erected to his memory on a wind-swept hill of South Georgia, I meditated on his great deeds. It seemed to me that among all his achievements and triumphs, great as they were, his one failure was the most glorious. By self-sacrifice and throwing his own life into the balance he saved every one of his men—not a life was lost —although at times it had looked unlikely that one could be saved.

His outstanding characteristics were his care of, and anxiety for the lives and well-being of all his men.

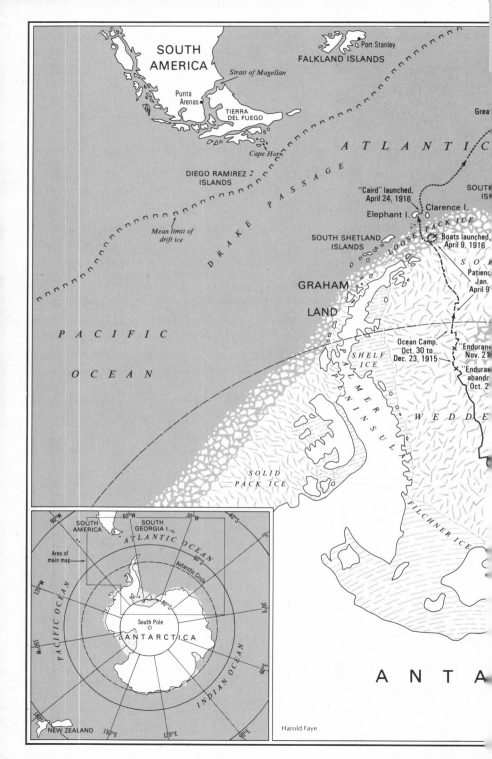

SOUTH AMERICA

Port Stanley
FALKLAND ISLANDS

Strait of Magellan

Punta Arenas

TIERRA DEL FUEGO

Cape Horn

DIEGO RAMIREZ ISLANDS

Mean limit of drift ice

ATLANTIC

Grea

"Caird" launched, April 24, 1916

Elephant I.   Clarence I.

SOUTH IS

DRAKE PASSAGE

LOOSE PACK ICE

SOUTH SHETLAND ISLANDS

Boats launched, April 9, 1916

GRAHAM LAND

S O

Patienc Jan. April 9

PACIFIC OCEAN

Ocean Camp, Oct. 30 to Dec. 23, 1915

"Enduran Nov. 21

SHELF ICE

"Endura abando Oct. 2

P E N I N S U L A

M E R

W E D D E

SOLID PACK ICE

FILCHNER ICE

A N T A

Inset map:

90°W   60°W   30°W

SOUTH AMERICA   SOUTH GEORGIA I.   40°S   0°

ATLANTIC OCEAN

Area of main map

60°S   Antarctic Circle   30°E

120°W

PACIFIC OCEAN   80°S   30°E

South Pole

A N T A R C T I C A

150°W   60°E

INDIAN OCEAN

180°   90°E

NEW ZEALAND   150°E   120°E

Harold Faye